To Sheila

Enjoy

John Twz

9/9/22

THE

SCIENCE

OF

BUSINESS

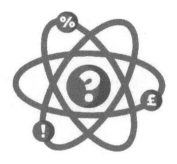

Why science holds the answers
to our business problems

Justin Turner

Published by AskJT Ltd

First edition printed by Mixam UK Ltd in the United Kingdom 2022.

Cover design: Lewis Rickman.
Typesetting: Matthew J Bird. Edited by: Steven Holmberg

A CIP catalogue record of this book is available from the British Library.

ISBN (Paperback): 978-1-73-967200-3
Imprint: Independently published

For further information about this book, please contact the author at: scienceofbusiness.co.uk

For Benji, James, and Sue

Contents

Introduction

My son received the most fantastic gift for his birthday. It was a kit that allows you to create poo smells and capture them in test tubes and bags. You can then release the smell at the time and place of your choosing. Wow! Genius!

Not so sure if Mum was so keen on the idea.

The kit is about encouraging kids to discover and explore science. Children are fascinated by poo, it's a fact! The kit appealed greatly to my son and he couldn't wait to try the experiment.

We often encourage children to give science a go, perhaps by making slime or creating a marble run. There are plenty of toys and games out there that engage children with scientific principles. Yet after GCSEs, many of us give up the study of science and think our journey with science ends. Yet, it's all around us! We're being influenced by it every day, and our scientific journey doesn't end at school, whether we like it or not. So maybe we just need to find something to rekindle the excitement we once had when creating poo smells!

But why write an entire book about science in business?!

I want to capture all of my own enthusiasm and passion, not just the smell of a great big ripping fart! I want to share my genuine love for business education and aim to capture it in the words I write. I hope to reacquaint you with the delight in science we felt when we were kids.

The book was born out of the frustration I witnessed. My clients were struggling as they desperately looked for answers to their business dilemmas.

For example, a client once said something startling to me, and it made me realise how we could benefit from better education about the potential impact of science on our businesses.

"I hate my staff!" he declared.

Strong words! I've been employing people for nearly 20 years and it has had its moments, and I certainly hope those four words will never leave my mouth. But I get it – dealing with staff is challenging! So how could science help this client? How can science assist business managers and owners to create a successful and harmonious workplace for themselves and their staff?

In this case, it comes down to the reality that managing people involves the application of social science. That's a type of science, yet most people don't understand it well enough to utilise it.

So why should you read this book? When looking for answers, it's not that hard to pick up a business book or read something online. But they rarely highlight and explain the science *behind* the subject matter. It's not made clear that we're learning something from *science*. Therefore, I've created this book to give you some immediate ideas based on existing scientific knowledge that will challenge the way you make decisions.

So many business books only paint pictures of tech startups with overnight success or multi-million dollar enterprises. For most of us, this is neither a dream nor what we truly want in our lives. Our battle is building something strong without having access to all the resources a larger company has. For me, running a business is not about creating a multinational but instead about building something solid and sustainable that provides me a flexible living for me and my family.

This book is written so that you can dip in and out of it. Each chapter is generally a stand-alone story or idea. The science in each chapter will give you principles as well as applicable ideas for change. The book is the culmination of my years of reading, learning, and observation, plus the resulting knowledge from all the trial and error of running a small business!

It should be a light read, yet one full of substance. And don't worry, I'm not going to get all geeky with too many graphs and citations and stuff like that. My aim is to educate you in the simplest way possible on what science can teach us about business, and how you can apply it.

The very design of this book is an example of what I mean. In modern society, we are visually overstimulated, so by looking at the science of design I can give this book the best possible chance of success. The book is printed using a Serif font. "So what?" you might say. Well, there is science behind the use of Serif fonts. They are proven to help guide your eye and to maximise readability. I've even considered the colour of the book cover and how the brain will interpret it. I've used a contrast checker to ensure the cover font colours work against the background. I've created a symbol to create a mental connection with the book. Everything I've mentioned in this paragraph is science. The key is knowing how to apply it to our everyday business and personal lives.

There's a lot of science out there, and it's complex. Business people are busy people, and I recognize that it's hard to know where to look for help and that it can be hard to apply the ideas we find. I'm hoping that this book will be an easy starting point for you. I'll share some ideas and explain why they help and how you might implement them. I'm not ashamed to declare that there is science out there that will change your entire outlook! People often briefly mention science in other books, seminars, etc., but no one sings from the rooftop about why it actually works! That's what this book is going to do.

About Me

Why should you listen to me? The answer is found in my strange career path.

I started my first business in 2004, and goodness me, I made some mistakes. I was green around the ears, a young man who made it up as he went along.

My first business was a web development business that closed just before its 10th birthday. It wasn't the roaring success I'd hoped to build, and the bad days outweighed the good. The credit crunch in 2009 was the death knell for the business as it didn't have the robustness to weather such a massive storm. We racked up multiple bad debts and some of our more prominent clients went bust.

Around 2011 I realised something had to give. I started looking for other opportunities to earn some much-needed income. I came across the opportunity to become a CPD (Continuing Professional Development) trainer for capital allowances tax claims on commercial property. My role was to go into firms of solicitors and accountants and teach them about making these claims on behalf of their clients. They could then earn CPD points for simply listening to me talk.

Although I enjoyed the CPD training, it wasn't paying the bills. So I asked friends and business contacts to keep their ear to the ground for opportunities. Then one day a friend asked if I'd like to help him set up a letting agency. Within a short amount of time the business had premises and staff and I'd become the Financial Director.

In 2010 I'd encouraged my fiancé (now my wife) to retrain as a bookkeeper. She was unhappy as a teacher, so after she chose to leave her teaching career behind, I helped her set up her own small bookkeeping business. But by the end of 2011, we were expecting our first child and her maternity leave was looming. She decided to leave her business in my capable hands, whilst she spent time taking care of our newborn son. I was already a dab hand with bookkeeping, as I had managed a struggling business and its cash flow problems for eight years. Together with my CPD training and my skills with managing client money at the letting agency, I had the confidence to take on the bookkeeping venture. Some personal demons with dyslexia had long left me feeling that I couldn't work in finance, but it turns out I couldn't have been more wrong!

My little bookkeeping business unexpectedly evolved into another love of my life (after my wife and children, of course). When my wife returned from maternity leave, the business she had left behind had become a fully fledged accountancy business.

I also picked up consultancy work, and I couldn't believe it – I was paid to fix other people's business problems! Not just paid but handsomely paid! All those mistakes and heartache I'd had in my first business meant I had a wealth of knowledge that I could pass on to other business owners.

As I encountered various challenges in my businesses throughout the years, I'd always had a thirst for knowledge. I began to understand where science was helping me. Rather than merely accepting failures and successes, I wanted to know why they happened in the first place, and scientific knowledge was my guide to understanding.

This knowledge was put to good use when Northumbria University approached me to lecture and teach various subjects, usually entrepreneurship and enterprise skills. I also helped deliver part of the government-backed educational scheme Help2Grow. The university was a great place to find a balance between the business world and my knowledge of science.

Fast forward to today. I am developing e-learning materials to help with business education, the letting agency is still going strong, and my accountancy business has become the success I always hoped for. The best part is that I love my job!

I may have a 20-year business career but I continue to learn something every single day. I don't expect this to end anytime soon and I can't wait to see what science will teach me tomorrow.

A Quick Note about the Book

I've related the concepts to personal stories to show that I'm not an all-knowing person and, in fact, I've made plenty of mistakes.

I've split the book into three sections.

The first section is about the guiding principles I've learned from science that have made big differences in my business life. Things such as understanding that science in business does exist, using data analysis, and utilising tools to reach my goals. This may sound complex but I've made it super simple for you to enjoy.

The second section is about the brain and people. There is a vast amount of psychology required in managing and building teams. If we can understand some of the basic principles of the brain and how people who work for us are wired, we can be better at managing them. Much of my success is about the people who support me. If I can understand them, then I can better support and help them. I'll show you how to unlock some of the power of the brain to put this into practice straight away.

The third section is about science in its practical applications. It's about how I've seen science used or how I've applied it myself in areas such as marketing, sales, innovation, and leadership. It's fair to say the last section contains the ramblings of my brain. It explores how I consider science in most settings and how I think deeply about cause and effect. And a little bit about how I experiment!

Of course there's crossover in the various sections. I aimed for a logical structure that helps you get the most you can from the book.

I genuinely believe that I've found a little niche for this book, and I'm excited to show you how science will be able to help your business.

1

Read lots, but consider carefully
Don't believe all the science you see

I read my first business book while an undergraduate at university called *Rich Dad Poor Dad* by Robert T. Kawasaki. It was a revelation on how to think about money. My only challenge was that it indicates you need a business to gain true success. People follow *Rich Dad Poor Dad* like the bible, but I've realised you need all sorts of knowledge in your arsenal to undertake the process of running a business. There are some great money lessons in the book. I've even given this book as a gift to people who then told me they wished they'd read it sooner.

Business books aren't always about taking what they say as gospel but rather providing you with ideas to create a form of balance. Over the years, I've read 100s of business books, and through my teaching at the university, I've read lots of journals and academic texts. We need to review all these business books with science in mind. I think, and I hope, you'll see some of the balance and complexity of running a modern business as you read this book.

Look at science and question the content. It's rare to read an article or book and get the whole answer. Usually, we need to experiment and measure the results of actions. There can be many moving parts, and fundamentally, humans don't like change. Quite often, changing something like how you manage a team takes time and patience. It's rare for an idea we implement to work the first time around.

The critical takeaway with any information is to absorb what you can and ask the following questions:

1. Is it relevant to me?
2. Is it backed with good quality scientific proof?
3. Do I have the skill to do it?
4. What other skills do I need?

Even in this book, I scratch the surface in order to stimulate thinking, but many ideas need you to expand your knowledge via further reading or research.

That term scientist – yes, I'm one of those. I don't wear a white coat or have a PhD or work in a field we would describe as science. Yet we are all scientists, especially those who own small businesses. We experiment all the time, and we're tapping into a wealth of knowledge.
By the way, not for one minute can I let you think all the ideas in this book are mine.

Mark Twain said it best:

> **There is no such thing as a new idea. It is impossible. We simply take a lot of old ideas and put them into a sort of mental kaleidoscope.**

There is nothing wrong with doing that – it's all I do during my teaching at Northumbria University. We take well-established research, apply it to some real examples, formulate it into a logical order, and then deliver it with different teaching techniques.

When we look at university study we view degree programs either as BSc (Bachelor of Science) or a BA (Bachelor of Arts). So if it's a BA degree, does that mean there's no science? Irrespective of degree classification, some form of science is always happening. After all, science is the study of the behaviour of the physical and natural world through observation and experiment. All academic papers contain an element of science, but also a brushstroke of artistic interpretation.

So, I'm hopefully taking you on a scientific journey of discovery to show you what's possible with the magic that is science in business. I see this book as a mental kaleidoscope of my learning over the years. A book I couldn't have written any earlier in my career.

Scientific Proof Isn't Everything.

You might be inspired by this book to look at every piece of science you can find. However, you need to learn something first. A great book by Ben Goldacre called *Bad*

Science teaches you how to be critical about scientific knowledge. He's a medical doctor and highlights why we need to be critical of scientific understanding. I don't object to people debating any subject areas in this book. After all, I'm a scientist; I must embrace the debate we have in the scientific community. Ben's book is excellent because he highlights that just because a scientific journal has been published, it doesn't mean it's good science. He explores other worthwhile things, such as what we can learn from failure and why you must publish failed scientific efforts.

Let me give you an example to cement this notion. Like many others, I suffer from bad skin, so one day my mum texted me a newspaper article about a particular probiotic that had been shown to improve skin conditions (thank goodness for mums). The claim in the newspaper was unbelievable! I was online looking for these magic pills, but I stopped before I pressed the checkout button – my scientific brain had kicked in. I found the study the newspaper had quoted and discovered the study had been conducted using only rats, and the number of rats in the study totalled only 12. The results had not been repeated, and I couldn't find any details about a control group. All this doesn't mean probiotics are ineffective, but this type of research is dangerous.

The scientists hadn't published the study in order to make headlines, but the newspaper wanted to sell papers, so it touted the study and thus became a purveyor of bad science. The scientist may have done the experiment to simply determine if a more extensive study or even a human trial might be beneficial. And they did what they should have done: they published in a scientific journal. But that study was never meant to be published in a widely-circulated newspaper and used as the sole source of a brazen claim!

You must check that what you read makes sense and has scientific rigour.

One of the best examples of bad science has been the overuse of OxyContin (an opioid pain medication) in the United States. It is dramatised by DisneyPlus in the miniseries *Dopesick*, which highlights what happens when bad science is rotten. It chronicles the true story of a horrendous yet legal drugs trade situation. Medical journal articles that didn't exist were referenced, graphs were changed, and medical literature was developed with the intent to mislead. If you ever watch it, think about it with your newfound scientific brain.

Remember, bad science is everywhere! Even my own observations and experience don't automatically make for good science so hopefully the studies I reference back up my statements and provide substance to my claims.

Part1 Scientific Principles
Scientific Principles

2

What science tells business!
Why science is important to businesspeople

Here's a quote that changed my life and turned my focus to science, and probably led to my writing this book:

There's a mismatch between what science knows and what business does.
Dan Pink

Scientists are often looked at in disdain, especially with regards to things we don't want to hear. Now, I happen to find it astounding what scientists have achieved. For example, they imagined, designed, built, launched, and flew the James Webb telescope 1.5million miles from Earth. I'd figure that most people would think that's pretty remarkable, no questions asked. Yet when it comes to, say, climate change, many people will disregard and even deride carefully analysed scientific data. This same problem is true in business. Why does some data get embraced and other data get tossed out the window?

Data is everywhere in our modern businesses. We live in an information-driven world, and many companies have data collection happening behind the scenes. However, all that data isn't being utilised effectively, and we can use science to remedy this. There is a big difference between data and information. We've certainly seen the appearance of many web applications endeavouring to profit from turning data into information. So how do we turn data into valuable information?

We need a scientific mechanism to measure the results of our actions.

Positive Results vs Negative Results

Businesspeople are driven to work out why positive or negative results are achieved. To understand the why's, I'm constantly looking to science.

Let me ask you to consider something:
How do you reduce the number of towels used by guests while staying in a hotel? Take a moment to really consider that for a moment or two.

In collaboration with Surrey University, Melvin Mak undertook a study of a 700-room hotel on the Canary Island of Fuerteventura. The study's goal was to increase the amount of re-usage of towels by hotel guests.

He decided to try different types of signs. He experimented with humorous messages, but they actually had a negative effect. He experimented with messages of doom and gloom, which actually worked, but they weren't the most successful of his trials.

What worked best was this: "Reuse me again tomorrow. Just like at home."
It increased the re-usage of the towels by 49.4%.

The study showed that every 10kg of towel wash used around 50 litres of water and 1.2 kilowatt hours of electricity. The most effective signage resulted in 56,474 fewer large towels and 69,616 fewer small towels being washed. The hotel reduced CO_2 emissions by 1,676 kg. All of this translated into significant cost-saving. The hotel uses towels. It spends money to manage them. This is all data, but without scientifically analysing the data, no change can happen. Mak's study implemented scientific techniques and a business was improved.

The experiment with the wording of signs is an exciting bit of research into usability. Such research attracts people in the web design world interested in making digital platforms more accessible. Have you ever noticed that all the action buttons on most websites are the same colour? What about the site's loading speed? Does it work well on a smartphone? Does it cater to people with disabilities? This is all about usability. I worked in the web industry and my colleagues and I talked about usability all the time, but I'd never really considered the other areas of science where it could apply.

It's fascinating to see how this scientific research can impact other domains. It's the same science, yet it's being used and thought about differently.

Incentives

Remember that quote at the start of this chapter? Dan Pink said it while giving a TEDTalk in 2009. One of the things he spoke about is the notion of incentives. Pink contended that incentives don't work in most business settings. Over the past several decades, other social scientists have also declared the ineffectiveness of incentives. For example, Sam Glucksberg experimented with Karl Duncker's "Candle Problem." In Duncker's original experiment, subjects were asked to affix a candle to a wall so that no wax would drip onto the table below it. They were given only a candle, a book of matches, and a small cardboard tray full of drawing pins. Subjects could take as much time as they needed. In Glucksberg's variation on the experiment, however, subjects were asked to finish the task *in the fastest time possible*. Some subjects were given cash incentives; other subjects were given no incentives.

The subjects with no incentives consistently outperformed the subjects with incentives.

In this study, no incentives = better results. Why? It comes down to the way our brains work. The Candle Problem requires an element of creativity, and incentives create a creativity block. So when considering incentives, it might be worthwhile to also consider how you prioritise creativity. I'm not saying that incentives never work, but a scientific approach to considering incentives clearly reveals why we need to think carefully about them.

I often hear my students suggesting incentives as motivational tools in problem-solving scenarios. "But why," I ask? They assure me that money always makes a difference, plus other companies use them, so it must be right. Oh really? You must have some science to back that up?

So why towels and incentives?

I've used two examples of science to make a point. Our business lives are full of opportunities, but we don't often consider and analyse in order to make the most of them. If asked how to increase towel re-usage, would you have implemented a scientific study to measure contrasting signage effectiveness? If we consider decision-making in business, there is likely to be established research and understanding. Yet we are either not searching it out or we are oblivious to its very existence.

3

The Power of the Moon
How to make great decisions

A friend of mine once posted on social media that there is a direct correlation between crime and the cycle of the moon.

"It's a full moon tonight! Watch out, everyone -- more crime happens on nights with a full moon!"

My friend isn't a nincompoop. He's a well educated and intelligent man. He was sharing the hypothesis that since the moon affects the tides of the oceans, it must also affect humans, who are made up of 60% water. He even had statistics about crime rates to back up his claim. So, what should we make of my intelligent friend's hypothesis?

Let me introduce you to Occam's Razor. In short, it is the principle that the simplest solution is often the best solution because it avoids unnecessary complexity. It has long been a principle in philosophy but it has also been a guiding principle in science. And it can revolutionise your decision making.

Let's first apply it to my friend's idea. First of all, I think we can agree that proving definitively why crime rates might be higher during full moons is a difficult challenge. Rather than imagining scenarios involving the moon's gravitational pull and all the factors that stuff entails, I applied Occam's Razor instead. In other words, is there a simpler answer? Well, what about the fact that when there's a full moon, there's more light by which to see. That bike left out outside can suddenly be seen when there's a full moon on a clear night. A crime of opportunity! Moon's effect...or more light to spot things to steal?

If you have two solutions to an idea, try the simplest first. Yes, there are arguments that the application of Occam's Razor might not lead to the most accurate solutions. But the underlying concept is very valuable – rather than spending time and energy on complicated solutions, try to find the most straightforward answer before anything else. I certainly don't want to delve into a debate about lunar phases, the human body, and crime stats. For me, it's about common sense and simplicity, and I think the fundamental scientific principle of Occam's Razor can be applied effectively in the world of business.

How?
As managers and business owners, we are always making hundreds of decisions. The best decision makers use Occam's Razor all the time, even if they don't know it.

When they have a decision to make, they find the simple solutions and they don't overcomplicate things. If we go back to my example of towel re-usage and laundry costs, what would you have done? Perhaps replace all your washing machines with ones that are more energy efficient? A complex (and costly) solution. Would you have come up with the idea to simply make some signs to reduce the number of towels being washed every day?

It's fine to start somewhere, even with a complex solution. However, take the time to apply Occam's Razor and see if there's a simpler solution. Einstein's theory of relativity is a tremendously complex concept that fills pages and pages of proofs. Yet it fundamentally boils down to one single expression: $E=mc^2$.

You'll want to implement some of the ideas in this book, which will require you to make some decisions, so keep the principle of Occam's Razor in mind. Keep to that spirit of always looking for simplicity.

Timing a decision is critical

So now that you are of the mindset to look for simple solutions, let's talk about how to time them. Most of our decisions in small business are about making them quickly, as we go. We make many decisions on instinct. So I want to introduce you to some key concepts to help the process.

- Do you have the facts and reliable information to back up your solution to a problem? Look to science and reputable sources of knowledge. If the facts don't support what you are doing, stop for a moment and stand back. Then look for the simplest solution. Look for valid data in your business and create information from it.

🕸 Identify your most significant decision of the day and tackle it first. Your brain is fresh in the morning after sleep (the science of melatonin, a discussion I'll leave for my next book!) so take advantage of this. Deal with your most arduous task first. If you do this every day, over the long term, you will form the valuable habit of overcoming your most challenging tasks quickly. For more on this type of thing, read Brian Tracy's brilliant book *Eat That Frog*, which is full of great ideas to help you get things done and to form good habits.

🕸 Never make an important decision on an empty stomach. I'm not joking! A 2019 study by the University of Dundee showed that being hungry changes our decision-making processes. I'm sure you've heard the expression "hangry," and there's truth in it! If I have a difficult task or big decision, I often stop for some food first. I know I'll return refreshed afterwards. Some of the worst decisions I've ever made have been on an empty stomach.

🕸 Decision fatigue! We make around 35,000 decisions each day, but as the day wears on, the quality of the decisions deteriorates. I speak from my own experience! January is the worst month of my work year. Many people leave their tax returns to the last minute, so during January I work on many tax returns at the same time. This requires me to keep a vast amount of information in my head. This overload leads to changes in other parts of my life. My triathlon training usually goes out the window first. The family meal plan breaks down. The house gets untidy. In general, I struggle to achieve all my desired goals when I'm too fatigued from so many decisions. Have you ever noticed Mark Zuckerberg wears the same t-shirt? One less decision to make! In short, try to eliminate the number of decisions you make each day. Or at least be conscious when you've had a decision-heavy day, then ask for help or get other people to check your work.

Do the above ideas work when decisions are more complex?

When you have to make those BIG decisions that might significantly impact a business's future, I implore you to look at some other tools to assist you. To identify when you might need a more robust framework for decision making, consider if you have the following issues:

1. You don't even know where to start.
2. You can't see all the perspectives of everyone involved.
3. A solution is needed, but it's not clear.
4. The interpretation of the problem is seen differently by others.
5. You need to find quality information that doesn't exist.

I always hope that most day-to-day problems are easy to solve. But if you do have a larger project with a considerable degree of risk, then think about using a framework such as SMART. It's a tool used by the NHS and numerous other large organisations. It was developed in 1981 by George Doran, Arthur Miller, and James Cunningham as a way to set management goals and objectives. SMART stands for specific, measurable, attainable, realistic, and timely. Each letter sums up, more or less, everything you need to do when it comes to achieving a positive outcome to problems. You can also implement ADAPT, another decision-making framework I discuss in my chapter on innovation.

There is fascinating NHS documentation available online which highlights how you can use specific problem-solving tools. If you search "Quality, service improvement, and redesign (QSIR) tools by stage of project nhs" you will find a whole range of examples. These will help you consider larger problems more effectively. Why reinvent the wheel when the NHS has a whole range of examples waiting online to help you?!

As you will continue to find out, I love drawing on knowledge from other industries. When it comes to decision making, finding a solution from other sources gives you one less decision to make – and it's so simple!

4

Have you ever tried drinking a litre of beetroot juice?
Data, analytics, and information interpretation

As a keen triathlete, I found a scientific study that told me that if I drank a large amount of beetroot juice, it would increase nitrates in my body and thus improve blood oxygenation. I saw this as a quick win because without doing any more training I could get a benefit from drinking this magic elixir. Even better, supermarkets sold it. The only issue was that I was required to drink 500ml the night before and 500ml two hours before racing. For those who don't know, beetroot juice is an acquired taste – and I didn't have a taste for it. Gagging, writhing, and a bloated feeling followed. Don't let me tell you about the public urinal and how someone advised me to visit a doctor!

After drinking gallons of this rank juice, I told a friend that I just couldn't go on. She said, "You know, there is a company that makes a special shot of concentrated beetroot juice, especially for sport. You drink one 70ml shot, and it's equivalent to 500ml of juice." I was close to tears at this news – my beetroot torture would end! Ever since, I've simply drank the shot, which doesn't really taste that bad.

So does it work? Yes, it does, and it's one of the few foods that scientists have proven to give a sporting advantage. Sports nutritionists agree that your overall diet plays a more significant role in recovery and building muscle, but I had found a quick win that actually worked.

Despite the struggles with my beetroot juice habit, I had realised science might have more to teach me. Similar to how my study into beetroot juice developed, I searched out any articles that chronicled the collection of some form of data and the subsequent careful analysis of it. I wanted to read about the transformation of data into information – information that was easily understandable. Hang on a minute! I must have data!

I observed that my smartwatch was tracking all kinds of stats during each of my triathlon training sessions, but I hadn't been considering how they could help me:

- I noticed a piece of data called cadence (how many steps per minute (spm) you take during a run). I was taking 157 spm. I found an athlete named Jack Daniels who researched this in 1984, and he showed that 180 spm were ideal. I started on a mission of change, and the following season my run times improved and I felt more comfortable. Bags of research were available to help me once I took note of the data that I was only taking 157 spm.

🏵 I learned about FTP (Functional Threshold Power). FTP is how many watts of power I can produce through a bike pedal over an extended time. I could suddenly track this during my interval sessions, so I was always trying to push the intervals into the higher numbers.

🏵 I could track how many carbohydrates I was consuming when racing. I hadn't known that this was useful. Did you know the body can only absorb 60g of carbohydrate per hour? My nutrition now involves gels and drinks that give me that exact number.

So why am I telling you this? You may have thought I was telling you about business. Well, the importance of data is the key message, and data is everywhere.

New and existing data collection

My business life is the same as my triathlon training. I can tell you things like:

🏵 How many clients are on the books
🏵 At what rate we win them
🏵 How long it takes them to accept a proposal
🏵 How many visitors go to our website
🏵 How much work we have outstanding

- ❀ How many hours are spent on each client and by which member of staff
- ❀ Who opens our email newsletters & which links they click.

I have all the financial data, like profit and loss, balance sheet, aged payable, and debtors. My job is to apply some science to all that data and turn it into useful information. If it's already helpful information, I can do something about it.

Let's take one example: people who owe us money. We refer to this in accounting as aged debtors.

"How can we get our clients to pay us faster?" a client asked me.

"Do you know the average time it currently takes them to pay?" I enquired.

"Not a clue, that's why I'm asking you!"

"Easy! You have great bookkeeping records so let's use a super simple ratio called debtor days."

We discovered in about five minutes it was taking 56 days for the customers to pay. All of a sudden we had information that was meaningful. I suggested we should target 30 days to collect the payments.

"Let's try giving your customers the option to pay by bank card. And what about direct debit for those recurring payments? Have you sent out reminder statements? What about reminder emails or even a call?"

Prior to the client utilising a ratio, they didn't have precise numbers, but now we could compare and measure the results of my proposed solutions.

I hope you see where I'm going. The example is simple: we turn existing management accounting data into a ratio, and that ratio then serves as useful *information*. Then we generate even more data: How long does it take to chase debt? What are the staff costs? Can things be automated? (Yes, they can!) Invoice reminders can be sent automatically; direct debit systems can be used to collect the money automatically. We can use software to automatically generate the debtor days ratio. Once we are aware of all these types of things, we then just need to decide on the right option. Most importantly, that chosen option allows us to measure against what was happening before.

Many of the solutions I come up with involve apps. I love an app! Many of the apps I add to my business need to have built-in analytics tools. The analytics mean that I don't have to start analysing datasets as it's being done for me as I go.

You need to think carefully about technology, so let me give you an example. A friend had a business problem and asked me for help:

"We are trying to price staff at £60 per hour, but the business is only achieving £30 per hour, and we've run out of capacity," he explained.

I suggested he set up all his projects into a time-tracking process whereby the staff notes on a paper timesheet the time taken for each job. Within one month, we had data: some of the jobs were taking so much time the business was struggling to achieve even £10 per hour on specific projects.

He runs an advertising business, and his skilled staff are more valuable than a £10 per hour rate.

As the company expanded, he found it difficult to keep track of what everyone was working on. The new process that I suggested suddenly gave him much-needed insights. He then spoke to his clients to secure new contracts and he incorporated budget limits.

These changes posed little risk to his business because he was already losing money on some jobs. Plus, much-needed capacity would be freed up if a client left following a price rise. That said, I don't think he lost any clients, as they knew they were on a fantastic deal, possibly to the point of taking advantage of the situation!

At first, this system was just a paper exercise with someone inputting the data into a spreadsheet. A software solution was soon implemented to track projects with in-built reporting. There was no more time-consuming analysis on spreadsheets and instead there were on-demand reports.

By the way, starting with paper recording kept us true to Occam by keeping the solution simple. Complexity was added later with the addition of software, once we had tested and measured.

How we approach a problem

Going back to the theme of the beetroot juice…

My message is that there is often a better way of doing things. I was trying to consume one litre of juice in under 24 hours. While we can always look to science for answers, how we implement those answers can make all the difference. Some enterprising company did just that – they saw the beetroot research and created their unique beetroot shot.

And if we consider my friend's hourly rate business problem…

On the one hand, it's tempting to rush off and implement a software app, but this comes with challenges, such as the setup time, staff training, cost, etc. On the other hand, tracking something on paper for one month and then analysing it via a spreadsheet is very time-consuming, and what happens if the data comes back to show there was no problem in the first place? In either case, you run the risk of wasting huge amounts of time, resources, and money, possibly on a solution to a problem that didn't exist in the first place. Sometimes we think we may have found a great solution, but the *best* solution might not be the *first* one you think of.

Don't be deterred if you haven't found the right solution. As business people, we tend to have a gut feeling about what we suspect is the root cause. And, of course, there is science in gut feelings. A fascinating study in *Nature* magazine shows that humans pick up on hidden information and draw on past experiences. We just need the data to back it up and then base decisions on this data. The *Nature* study shows that sometimes those gut feelings can't be relied upon, so we need information to guide us.

Let's explore time

I love the concept of using data to explore how the usage of time is so important. One can easily forget that how time is used is very valuable data.

One day I appeared with a stopwatch in the office. I wanted to time how long it took to process a purchase invoice. We opened the envelope, typed the contents into the accounts software, numbered it, and filed it.

Questions were buzzing around my brain. What if we could get the supplier to email directly into our accounts software? What if this software could read the invoice and do some data entry for us? What if the system was HMRC compliant and we didn't need to keep a copy on paper? How much did it cost to print a purchase invoice when it was emailed to us?

Remember what I was saying about questioning things? Why was I doing all this? A software company had approached me, telling me they could save me hours in staff time. They offered a technology solution that automated invoice processing. I didn't take the company's claim at face value because I knew every business was different, and just because it works for one company, it doesn't mean it'll work for me. Plus, was it actually a simple solution?

I collected some data, and then I ran my own experiment tracking a piece of paper. We found that certain complex invoices of multiple pages could take an hour for someone to process. So in order to compare with my own data, we took a trial of the software and gave it a go with the stopwatch in hand! Wow! It saved us an enormous amount of time. The software was so clever it could even identify the purchase invoice to a bank line and auto reconcile.

The app saves hours of time each week, but I came to realise that some of the automation features like auto approval were a step too far. A skilled bookkeeper brings unique experience and ultimately prevents errors. That's more data: how many transactions a computer gets wrong versus what a real person achieves.

Like I did in my triathlon training, I've taken the measuring mantra into the business world. Data science is fascinating when we look at how much untapped data we have at our fingertips.

Where to start?

Why not work out what data you have in your business already? I promise it's there waiting to be found.

Here are some ideas about where you can find useful data:

- How long does it take to make a sandwich?
- What is the error rate of the cash in the till at the end of the day?
- How many buttons are pressed on a till, or how long does it take to process a card transaction?
- For a web business, how long does a web page take to load? Which pages are the ones where people leave your website?
- For manufacturing businesses, what is the defect rate? Which lines are the most profitable? How many components per item? What is the stock turn?

Try writing down the five biggest problems you have in your business, then see what data might exist to assist you. Maybe there's data that simply isn't being collected and could really help you if identified and analysed.

I promise you will have numbers in your business, and once you find them, see if you can turn that data into information. Then make simple decisions based on that information.

What have I learned?

Here are some quick takeaways from things I've learned over the years:

- I love technology, and in my business there is always software busily working away to reduce the boring bits. It's there to save time. It has helped keep my team engaged with the more exciting work. Yet, as the years went by, we had such an extensive suite of software that it became a staff training problem.

New starters felt overwhelmed and lost in the ocean of software. Rather than training them to be bookkeepers we were having to train them on using the software. Technology is not necessarily a better way of doing things, and we were exchanging one problem for another.

- Batching jobs together is faster. For example, making sandwiches can be achieved faster if all the rolls are pre-sliced rather than doing one every time a customer enters the sandwich shop.

- Making money is easy…as if! There are only three ways to make more money. It's simple! Sell more, increase prices, or cut costs. If you don't know where to start with your data analysis, then these three things should be your starting place. They'll keep you focused.

- Management accounts are full of helpful information. You have to produce figures to pay your taxes, so start using this data to run your business. Think about KPIs (Key Performance Indicators) or ratios. How can you turn data into an easily digestible number? Staff members can struggle to understand financial reports, but KPIs and percentages provide them with much-needed insight in ways they can understand.

- Start with a piece of paper! I felt pretty vindicated when Tokyo University came out with a study that showed working on paper showed higher levels of brain activity and made people more likely to recall information. Working out how data flows through an organisation is best done with pen and paper. Using a quick flowchart or mind map will quickly show you where all the points of data collection are happening.

Your business is generating data all the time so make sure you don't waste this valuable commodity. The next question is knowing how to focus on the most important areas...

5

80/20 Rules the Roost
Standard distributions & statistics

80% of beer is drunk by 20% of the people.
Jack Sparrow, *Pirates of the Caribbean*

Pareto's principle (named after the Italian economist) is the 80/20 rule. Pareto observed that 80% of wealth was held by just 20% of the population. He did this by looking at the percentage of land ownership in Italy. He discovered that 80% of the land was owned by just 20% of the population.

This principle applies to all sorts of things. For example, 80% of the seeds sown result in only 20% of all germinated plants. When you start looking you suddenly discover all the different situations where the principle applies.

Pareto's principle is a fascinating concept for entrepreneurs and managers. Pareto analysis is a formally recognised method of analysing data and yes, it can apply to *your* business.

For example, you might discover some of the following:

- 80% of your income comes from 20% of your clients
- 80% of the time you spend at work is on 20% of your clients
- 80% of your company's income is generated by 20% of your staff
- 80% of social media engagement comes from 20% of the posts
- 80% of sick days are taken by 20% of the staff
- 80% of your supplies come from 20% of your suppliers
- 80% of accidents are caused by 20% of hazards

Let's use my business as an example. Our bookkeeping service takes up 80% of the time we spend with clients. However, the service only generates 20% of our income. Why? Well, we can't charge as much, so our margin is tighter. However, the quality and standard of the bookkeeping work feeds into the other services the business offers. Earlier in the book, I discussed data and the use of software to automate purchase invoices, and it is time in this area that I'm trying to improve.

Over the years, I've used automation and machine learning to optimise the service in order to change the bookkeeping model. With regards to staff costs, you shouldn't forget the administration role (which isn't fee earning), chasing debtors, managing the client onboarding, meeting new clients, etc. These are all things that factor into the 80/20 principle. It would be a mistake to say 80% of the staff are unproductive, as this isn't the case. It's just that we haven't factored in some of the hidden costs.

Maybe you need to consider these hidden factors in your own business.

So what can you do with it?

In the last chapter, I discussed all the excellent data we have in our businesses. It can be overwhelming when we start thinking about it but guess what? You don't need to look at <u>all</u> the data:

80% of the helpful information is generated by 20% of the data!

With this in mind I had earlier suggested you write down your five most significant problems. Why? I was trying to direct you towards the 20% of data that is worth analysing (that is, the data that makes a significant difference to your business.) I use software tools to collect and analyse data on a constant basis. I've realised that although we might not have a problem today, we might have one tomorrow, so I always gather data. A metric or graph that I pay little attention to now might be something I want to look at in the future.

My message is this: you should identify the 20% factors and prioritise them. One of my team members did this exercise with our client list to see which client represented the highest turnover as a percentage. Sure enough, there it was: the 80/20 split.

My business tracks time and analyses how much time we spend on clients. We tend to work on fixed fees, but sometimes a complex case can arise that suddenly absorbs more time than we expected. We use this information to adjust our prices to ensure we're fighting against the 80%. We set alerts on client projects for when we think they might overrun on time or for when something comes out of the woodwork to change our expectations. Our time analysis allows us to inform the client that we have to agree on additional work.

Once an opportunity has passed and work is complete, it is too late to approach the client for additional fees. Plus, it's far easier to tell a client that we've only quoted them for 4 hours of work yet we've tracked 3 hours and 37 minutes so far and might go over the budget.

Some analysis I did also shows that 80% of our new work comes from 20% of all client referrals. After doing some research, I found all kinds of further examples from marketing. When we send out an email newsletter, we have loads of stats from open rates, link clicks, etc. As a result, I can identify, for example, that the same 20% of clients click the links in the email newsletter every month.

You'll soon determine your own critical numbers and how the 80/20 rule guides you.

So how does all this fit with maths and science? Does it work?

Statistics

To prove that all this works, I'm going to quote some great quality information from YouTube. Yes, that well known source of scientific information. Bear with me.

My kids watched a Mark Rober video on how to win a game of Guess Who 96% of the time. More utter rubbish on YouTube…or so I thought! The video quickly dove into the subject of statistics and examined how results for things like exam grades tend to fall into a standard bell curve distribution (otherwise known as a normal distribution). In the example of exam grades, there will be a small proportion of students who achieve the highest grades and a small proportion who will achieve the lowest grades, but the vast majority of students, around 68%, will be somewhere in the middle.

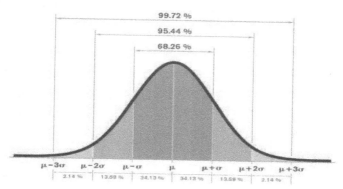

From my school boy maths I had always been familiar with a bell curve. I also used this type of graph during my university teaching to explain the adoption of new technology into the marketplace.

So you've noticed the largest proportion of a standard distribution is 68%. But it left me wondering why I was always finding 80/20 splits and not 68/32 splits in my business.

Did my school teachers teach me something that doesn't work?

The short answer is that the maths is sound. When we are specifically dealing with simple systems, the bell curve applies perfectly. I use the words "simple system" to describe situations with limited outcomes, such as height in the general population or the rolling of two dice. For example, in the case of rolling dice there are 11 possible outcomes from 36 different combinations. Furthermore, at the extreme ends of the spectrum there is only 1 way to gain the values of 2 and 12. However, to gain the value of 7 there are 6 combinations of the dice that can reach that outcome.

		Dice 1					
		1	2	3	4	5	6
Dice 2	1	2	3	4	5	6	7
	2	3	4	5	6	7	8
	3	4	5	6	7	8	9
	4	5	6	7	8	9	10
	5	6	7	8	9	10	11
	6	7	8	9	10	11	12

The mean value of outcomes refers to the highest number of combinations. Hence they are more probable.

In my example games of Guess Who there is only a limited range of outcomes (only 24 characters) so a bell curve will likely show you something meaningful. In other words, the data will fall into the pattern of 68% making up the majority. The games of Guess Who followed a *simple* formula and therefore the number of outcomes was limited.

However, in our businesses the ranges of data or the number of potential outcomes will be much higher in many situations. That's because the variation from the mean is far greater. The system in your business isn't simple but rather it is *complex*. In complex systems, you will tend to see the 80/20 effect reveal itself. For example, the Guess Who results changed for Mark Rober only once he applied a complex system (game strategy) to his game playing. Results that are similar to what we'll see in our own complex businesses began to appear: 80/20. The key is that a game of Guess Who has limited outcomes until we apply the complex game strategy. With all this in mind, from a statistical point of view you should therefore expect 80/20, not the normal distribution of 68/32, to show up in your business.

Don't worry too much about the maths (I'm not here to teach you about standard deviations, means, and probabilities). I just want you to understand enough to know that 80/20 is completely sound for business applications.

So how did Mark Rober win that even higher number of 96% of Guess Who games as per the claim in the video? I did promise at the start of the book I'd not get too geeky so I'm not going to fully explain. Suffice it to say that there's another bit of maths at work (the law of large numbers) which means that as you play more games, the average probability of winning increases. And Mark Rober played a *lot* of games.

Part 2 The Brain & People
The Brain and People

6

The Swimmer with One Arm
The science of habits & self doubt

There was a moment in my life where my perspective on self doubt changed.

I was approached before a triathlon race by someone wearing a large overcoat. As usual I was super early for transition to open at 6am. (Transition is the place where you leave your bike and move from one discipline to another.) This other keen bean was obviously just as anxious as I was to test out the 14 degree water ahead of our 7:45am start. Or maybe he had a date with half a litre of beetroot juice? It was the end of September, and it was touch and go whether the swim element would go ahead due to the unusually low water temperature.

"Can you help me? I don't know how to sort out my kit in transition as this is my first triathlon," spoke a voice.

"Yes sure, let me give you a few pointers. Are you looking forward to the event?" I said.

"I'm super nervous," he admitted.

"You've got nothing to worry about, this is a wonderful sport. The people are so friendly," I said encouragingly.

"Well it's just I've only got one arm and I'm really nervous about the swimming."

F**k me! I'd not realised with him wearing such a big jacket that he was missing an arm. Wow! What incredible courage to even contemplate swimming in a race environment. I didn't show my shock and gave out some more pearls of wisdom.

"Just enjoy it! Make sure you acclimatise to the water, start the swim at the back and not in the pack, and take your time," I said.

If only I could have followed my own advice. But that's a different story!

So how did he do? He came last. Slowest swimmer, slowest biker, but I don't think he was the slowest runner. I decided to find him at the end.

"Did you enjoy it?" I asked.

"Yes, I loved every minute and I'd do another one," he said with a huge grin.

So he came last, he definitely wasn't the best, but he enjoyed it and wanted to do more. Who ever said you need two arms to swim or to compete in a race? It's all just about the self doubt in your brain. If you set a goal then you can surely reach the end.

It was at that moment that I learned how self doubt will stop you in your tracks unless you challenge it. More than that, it showed me that having a goal to complete something is very powerful. Finally, it revealed something about the perception of situations: you might hold one particular perception that might not be the same one held by someone else.

My own perceptions of situations have held me back. They have resulted in my belief that I couldn't do something. Let me give you a small example.

"I feel like I've been a bit lazy recently!" I said to my friend Mark.

He couldn't contain himself and burst out laughing.

"Justin, lazy is not a word I could ever use to describe you. Have you ever thought it might be because you're not hitting your goals, thus leaving you feeling like you aren't achieving what you set out to do?"

It had never crossed my mind that the perception of not fully achieving my goals was making me feel like I was being lazy.

This was hammered home on another occasion when I was asked to make an introduction of myself in a social media group. I wrote some bits and bobs about my life that seemed of no great importance. However, the replies were all along the lines of "Wow, you have so much energy!" I had never thought of myself as someone with lots of energy. It was a perfect example of the contrast between how I perceived myself and how others perceived me.

All that energy I have can be a little hard to control. I've now realised that I always need any goals in my life to come with a deadline. This allows me to expend energy on the appropriate things.

I work better if I'm under pressure; I'm one of those nightmare people who leaves things to the last minute. However, it's just part of the process I use in order to produce my best work. (More about this and what I've learned about how my brain works later in the book.)

The research is out there to back up the importance of goal setting. People who set goals are better motivated, have higher self-esteem, and have more self-confidence and autonomy. There is an established connection between goal-setting and success.

How I've Used This

I read about an idea called "90 days of massive action" in a book written by Michael Heppell, a bestselling business author.

I decided to pick a project once a year that I'd commit to for 90 days. It was usually a New Year's resolution, but not always. I gave myself permission to carry on with it or bin it. This is a story about two of those little projects that ended up becoming huge loves of my life.

Around the start of July five years ago, I announced to my wife that I would attempt a triathlon. She was incredibly supportive and encouraged me to do it. I had always stayed away from the idea of doing a triathlon because I'd dislocated my shoulder twice and didn't think it would be possible. I often suffered from shoulder pain, and there was weakness around the joint, but I felt it was time to test the water. If I didn't do it then, I probably never would.

To keep me motivated, I set the goal of doing a triathlon at the end of September. (A few years later I met the one armed swimmer at this same annual event). Little to my wife's knowledge, I'd actually entered an open water triathlon. The only issue was that I couldn't do front crawl, so off I went twice a week to the pool. The pool had the hosepipe on standby as I was swallowing rather a lot of the water during the first few weeks (at least my hydration levels were being maintained!) However, I carried on and soon found myself buying a wetsuit, training in the local lake, and being able to swim 1000m front crawl.

The big day in September arrived and, though I was towards the back of the field, I finished. Fast forward five years and I'm happy to call myself a true triathlete. I even picked up an age category win at my club championship awards and a 2nd place podium finish in my age category at an event in Canada.

Of course, rather than making the shoulder worse, doing triathlon has strengthened it, and I rarely notice any discomfort now. Not only that, but when I look in the mirror I see a chap who is lean and 15kg lighter than when he started. What started with 90 short days has turned into an obsession and love for a sport.

Shrugging off self-doubt

Following my first triathlon, I started to think about all the things I didn't think I could do. I remember being told at school that because I was dyslexic I'd never be able to learn a language or play an instrument. So now it was time to learn French!

A quick internet search told me 90 days was all you need to learn a language. Just to clarify: do NOT believe everything you read on the internet. I started using an app and after 90 days I had some phrases but I was nowhere near able to speak the language.

Undeterred by my failure, I hired a French language tutor named Séréna. In our first meeting, I explained the feedback I'd heard from my teachers at school.

"Bof, I will get you to a fluent level, but it will take three years," said Séréna in her very direct Parisian way.

The first six months were horrific. I didn't enjoy it at all. After a year, though, things were starting to happen. After

18 months, I realised we were no longer speaking any English in the lessons, just French. Some time later, I realised I wasn't needing to translate what Séréna said to me, I was simply understanding it.

Today I can speak French fluently. I read French novels and I can have a debate in the French language. I achieved my goal! (And I have continued to learn more to this day.)

The matter of dyslexia always left a niggling doubt in my mind. It shouldn't! There are loads of people who have dyslexia, and I've learned that they include some of the world's most successful business people. Furthermore, it has been shown that people who have overcome dyslexia are better at overcoming other difficulties.

Perhaps my childhood teachers thought the process of learning a language would be too challenging because of various classroom and school constraints. Perhaps they thought it was pointless because they thought I couldn't ever reach mastery. Perhaps my own memories and perceptions are skewed due to my age at the time and how many years have passed. Yet whatever happened, and wherever my self doubt came from, I needed to understand how to battle it.

It all comes back to the swimmer with one arm. Am I the best at triathlon or do I speak perfect French? Nope! Is this the best business book ever written? Nope! But do I actually have to be the best? Of course I don't and of course neither do you. It is only the tiniest percentage of a field that reaches the absolute top of its game. Accept that, and accept that the rest of us don't have to be perfect.

For example, I recently went on holiday to France and I was able to have a great, less than perfect chat with the people running the bar. It was a priceless human connection and I didn't need perfect French to make it happen.

Self doubt is a real obstacle to setting goals, and the fear that it creates is often why we don't do anything in the first place.

What I've learned

Once you've shrugged off your self doubt, you are ready to set some goals.

You'll already know that goal setting is a good thing, but there's more science to back up the approach. The brain is always looking for ways to reduce effort. If we do something for 90 days and develop a routine, the routine turns into a habit. This is a bit of an oversimplification of the concept but trust me: there is a lot of research to show it works. There's likely proof from your own life. Do you have a negative habit you'd like to get rid of? Well, how did it begin? Likely from doing something over and over again. It works the same way for positive habits.

The lesson here is that while sometimes 90 days isn't enough to complete a project it is a great way to get us started. It has been great for enabling me to shrug off my mental roadblocks and self-doubt. It has allowed me to explore my mind and create a determination within me that pushes me forward each day.

A study by BJ Fogg at Stanford University found that scaling back bigger efforts into smaller, more manageable ones can create dramatic shifts that endure. That's basically what I try to do. I make a small change and build it into my daily routine. A little bit of French practice and a little bit of triathlon training. I've also done this with learning the piano. The key is that I'm not trying to make all these changes in one huge shift. It is small shifts achieved over time that allow us to reach our ultimate goals.

If you need to change something in your business it could start with a mere 90 days. You'll be amazed. It's just important to do it in small, manageable chunks. Don't try to solve a problem with one massive effort – try 90 days.

In fact, the main content for this very book was written in a 90 day period. I'd already fostered other 90 day habits in my life so I knew the power of doing a little bit each day. When it came to editing and proofing, it easily became another familiar routine. I don't try to be a full time writer but instead divide the whole task into daily, short writing stints. The initial self doubt about whether I could be a writer has evolved into discovering a love for writing my little book, and it has allowed me to overcome my greatest fear and to tell myself, **"I'm not a dyslexic idiot!"**

7

The Injured Deer
Everyone is different

"**A**re you better working individually or in a team?"

I hate this question! Interviewers ask this question but have no idea why they are asking it. Neither the person asking the question nor the person answering it really understands.

You see, I'm an extrovert, so I need people around me to give me my mental energy. That interview question should exist in order to determine a personality type. Sorry, but the vast majority of us just don't have the foggiest. I'm 39 and it is only in the last 5 years I could have made a reasonable attempt at answering the question effectively. That said, I would have been safe anyway, as the interviewer wouldn't have understood why they were asking the question in the first place.

Now bear with me. I'm not going to tell you about magic crystals or the power of the sun giving us superpowers. I'm a man of science, after all, and this chapter will help you understand how your brain works. It will help you to understand others.

Before I start my story, I want you to do something for me. Cross your fingers or your arms. Now try to do it the opposite way. Doesn't that feel odd! Your brain has been wired in a particular way and it prefers doing things in that way. Here is another one: look in a mirror and move your eyes side to side. I'll bet you don't see anything. That's because your brain has filtered out the movement. Your brain is merely making guesses most of the time and then filling in the gaps.

So what does all this mean, and what can we do about it?

My Story of Discovery

Through a networking group, I was offered the opportunity to do a Myers-Briggs test, and about a dozen of us decided to team up. Since we'd clubbed together we were able to secure a great deal for a normally expensive exercise. Included were the test, results, 1-to-1 psychologist assessments, and a follow up training day. A tester came to the office and administered the test to me. The test scores were added up and we were given our results. Terrific, I thought, a load of letters – I was apparently an ESTJ. If I'm being honest, I had been a little sceptical about the whole thing, but little did I know a life changing experience was about to follow.

Next up was a psychologist who came to my office and asked me even more questions. Here's where things became fascinating. She gave me several insights into my personality, including the fact that, although the test measured me as well-organised, in actuality I do not tend to be adept at organisation skills. It's only because my powers of self-control and professional training overcome this tendency to disorganisation that I test as well-organised.

"You're not naturally well organised," she said.

Bang! She was on the money. I use diaries, project management software, lists, etc. to keep myself organised. So my Myers-Briggs result was changed by the psychologist from ESTJ to ESTP. During the same meeting, a question popped into my brain and I blurted it out.

"My wife thinks I'm dead inside as I never cry at films. Am I?"

"Why do you say that?" she asked, laughing.

I explained that I'd recently watched the film *Boy in the Striped Pyjamas* and not a tear was in sight. Through her own flood of tears my wife cried, "There is something wrong with you, you're dead inside!"

Her comment had been bothering me ever since. I could empathise with the horrible things portrayed on screen, but they couldn't bring me to tears.

"Of course you're not dead inside. In fact, it's completely normal for your personality type, and I can prove it. Your brain is wired more than most others to interpret facts. You score highly on the Myers-Briggs scale in this area. The 2nd World War happened a long time ago so your brain simply tells you there is nothing you can do to change the outcome. Moreover, you're watching a film – your brain perceives a fictional story and finds it hard to relate it to real life. You feel there's simply nothing you can do in the present to help those poor people and the boy in the striped pyjamas."

Wow! This was mind blowing, and there was still more to come.

The next phase was a training day, during which all of us who had done the test and the psychological assessment were put together in a room. The first letter of the Myers-Briggs indicator is either E or I. Extrovert or introvert, not too difficult to understand. Depending on which letter had been assigned to us, we were put into one of two groups. We were then given the task to draw a poster that advertised the upcoming arrival of a circus to our local town.

I was part of the extrovert group and mayhem soon ensued. Arguments over who would do the drawing, multiple people drawing at the same time, colour all over the place. The introverts, on the other hand, discussed how to undertake the task and elected a leader who would draw. They worked in silence as they reached various stages, always discussing what to do next.

The extrovert poster was full of colour, but it was messy and it lacked any details like dates and times. The introvert poster was less colourful, but it was tidy and it included key details such as location, dates, and times. Each group had worked in very contrasting ways. By the way, the contrast had been obvious early on by the noise coming from my group and the relative silence of the other group!

The task helped me begin to gather a deeper understanding of people. It was a real lesson to me about where introverts and extroverts draw their energy. Extroverts need others around them, whereas introverts need time to internalise their thought processes, often via periods of calm consideration. I've done this same exercise with 180 students in a lecture theatre and it's always a great way to reveal different personalities within a group.

The next task of the training day was about whether you were a Thinker or a Feeler (T or F). The task was this: "You come across an injured deer that has been hit by a car. Come up with a solution."

There were only two of us in the Thinker camp and we had the whole thing cracked in about 60 seconds. The other group were deep in conversation; there were sheets of paper with plans being drawn up.

"What's taking you so long?" we said, poking fun at the other group.

The psychologist replied, "Why don't you tell the other group your solution?"

"Get the local farmer to shoot the deer and end its suffering," I said.

The Feelers were shocked! But they soldiered on and proceeded to outline their comprehensive plan to get the deer to an animal hospital and care for it.

As we reached the end of the day, someone I'd known for a number of years said to me, "I've often found it difficult to relate to you, Justin, but now I understand your point of view." This person was essentially the opposite to me on the Myers-Briggs indicator.

Some of you might read about my approach to the deer dilemma and also be shocked, but the key thing to remember is we are all wired differently. Just because an approach is different doesn't mean it's wrong. I've also learned that it doesn't always mean my way is correct either. I've found, as well, that life events can change me. Having children, for example, has made me think in terms that are less black and white. My wife still isn't fully convinced I'm not dead inside, however. I'd bet most doctors and nurses fall into the feeler camp and thank goodness for that.

Make People & Teams Work

The Myers-Briggs experience has been very useful. The moment I walk into a room for a meeting I try to work out where people sit on the Myers-Briggs scale. If someone is a Feeler then it may be pointless trying to convince them of something using facts and figures. They will instead want to know about the benefits of things or how people react emotionally when they use a product or service. Introverts often have great points to make but they'll often be less likely to speak up in a meeting. I make a point to slowly draw introverts out or to engage them for their opinions later on a 1-to-1 basis. I'm now conscious that introverts are tremendous listeners so while they often stay quiet, they are the ones who leave with the best understanding. I encourage you to have a go at a Myers-Briggs test, but it's best to also do some research into what it all means.

Have you ever been in a meeting or worked in a team and thought that you were surrounded by idiots? (Someone even wrote a book with that title!) You don't need to read the book but the gist is that it's important to acknowledge that you're not surrounded by idiots. Rather, you're simply surrounded by people who are different. When it comes to managing a team, understanding how people tick gives you a much stronger starting point.

There is another academic theory named after psychologist Bruce Tuckman which describes how new teams go through different stages: forming, storming, norming, performing, and adjourning.

Our university teaching team consistently saw these stages occur when we assisted groups of students with successful team building. When a new member is introduced into a team or when a brand new team is created (the forming stage), everyone tends to be very polite. Following that, team members enter a stage where they don't yet know how to work with each other effectively. Though it sounds counterproductive, this storming stage isn't a problem. In fact, it's necessary. However, team members need tools to progress into the norming and performing stages. (When things start to work themselves out, followed by when the proper work starts to get done.)

The issue we encountered when assisting student groups was that too many only stormed – they never progressed to the norming stage.

To overcome this we utilised another testing methodology that we had become familiar with: Belbin. Belbin is a great tool and is used to measure how an individual will behave in a team environment.

We used it to help students create more effective business groups. The goal was to get past the storming stage of conflict and into the norming stage of resolution and mutual appreciation. Over the years we kept seeing groups collapse into mayhem rather than cohere into working teams. So we aimed to help students better understand their new teammates.

With this in mind, we brought in a guest lecturer who taught the students about personality types, and I organised a practical session on introverts and extroverts. During it all, we never allowed an entire group from the same degree course to form into one group. For example, no teams of only computer scientists or only businesspeople. Teams rarely succeed if everyone is the same, and if you have a computer scientist, a designer, a marketer, a business student, and a fashion student, you will have a far greater array of skills.

When I looked at the results from my own Belbin test, I discovered that I barely register in the "finisher" category but I rate high in the "starter" category. A starter type can be infuriating in a team environment, and I'm a great example. I'm the person who starts things yet never finishes them. (Much to my wife's annoyance! All those home projects...) Let's hope I get this book finished.

However, a business will never move forward without starters like me. The key is to ensure that your business also consists of some finishers. I explain this to my own team and ensure I work with people who can finish things off. For example, I saw the opportunity to bring in some proposal software and I worked 12hour days setting it up. I had no intention of or interest in using it day to day, so that fell to someone in my team who was much more detail oriented and much better at finishing. The software has been a huge time saver for the business and provides analytical data. But it never would have been implemented without me and it never would have been a roaring success without my finishers.

Everyone in my team has to do a Belbin test when they start their employment. It's part of the process to help them understand themselves but also to work more effectively with their colleagues. And especially to understand why I'm that infuriating starter who never finishes things.

To summarise, there are two ways you can use this information to your advantage:

1. Learning about yourself and your team. If you understand how people approach things you'll be better at managing situations. Knowing yourself helps you explain to people how you work best. I often tell my wife that I work better in a team rather than by myself. Though she looks at me quizzically, I am aware I'm an extrovert and need people to give me energy.

2. When you walk into a meeting or group, being able to put people into categories makes it easier to present information in the right way. The introverts in a meeting are thinking "Why won't the extrovert shut up and let me think" and the extroverts are thinking "those introverts mustn't understand because they aren't saying anything."

This was all brought into context when I was helping a client modernise his business. I got on with the Managing Director like a house on fire. He said to me, "It's funny how we get on so well." But it was no surprise to me. I replied, "I bet if you do a Myers-Briggs test you'll have a similar, if not the same, personality type as I do. Sure enough, he was more or less the same. The only exception was he's just on the introverted side of things, and I'm just on the extroverted side, so there's not much difference between us. We were more or less the same!

It's easy to work with people of the same personality type but it doesn't always make for the most effective team. Our perceptions of situations are similar and we go about completing our work in similar ways. But the most effective teams need a range of different personalities to provide balance and views which might be different to your own.

This particular anecdote is a great case in point. When we went on to look at the Managing Director's Belbin test he measured strongly as a "starter." He had long been complaining about how his team was often annoyed by his many ideas. But having developed an understanding of personality types, he's been more mindful of what he brings to the team. It allows him to know when to put forward ideas and when to hold others back for another day.

8

Becoming a Clairvoyant
Don't fall into a thinking trap

"I know what you are thinking," someone said to me recently.

"Wow! I didn't realise you had the power to read minds," I said, bemusedly.

Mind reading is an example of a thinking trap.

(I've italicised the names of key thinking traps for you to consider as you read the chapter.)

How on earth can you know what someone is thinking? I'm one of those annoying people who will point this out. I hear this type of thinking trap all the time in my business life. Comments like, "I think the client is really happy with our work" and "I think the supplier is going to raise their prices."

Do these comments have actual evidence to support them? I take issue with the word "think." The word "think" is dangerous because you're not stating a fact but rather a supposition. There's a big difference between the two. If you hear this kind of talk within your team, ask for evidence and ask people to tell you what they actually <u>know</u>. It's not about being nasty but rather about getting teams to base decisions on evidence rather than guesswork.

Creativity can be another thinking trap because it can sometimes lead us astray from our goals. We end up trying to solve things that don't exist. Of course, it's human nature to think creatively and innovatively. I've done some reading into the psychology of creativity and it's interesting to learn that when a human being is creative they get a boost from their brain's reward system. You might know this as the feeling of relief and achievement you get when you solve a difficult puzzle. The boost is extremely important for humans:

The fact that evolution has linked the generation of new ideas and perspectives to the human brain's reward system may explain the proliferation of *creativity* and the advancement of science and culture.
Professor John Kounios, Drexel University College of Arts and Sciences

However, creativity needs to have its place. The creativity thinking trap occurs when the desire to get a reward gets in the way of original goals. Sometimes we need to rein in our creativity and stay on track.

But it's not just creativity. We have been conditioned to many types of thinking traps. We hear from media pundits guessing what a politician will do next. This thinking trap is *fortune-telling*. Those pundits cannot actually know anything for certain, yet their words are often taken seriously. If they can accurately read a politician's future then I suppose they could give me the winning lottery numbers, right?

My wife sometimes does what I'll call *all or nothing thinking*. She gets a tiny bit of criticism for something but then proceeds to say to herself, "I'm terrible at my job!" She's human like the rest of us and has merely made a minor error, but she allows her brain to go quickly down a one-way street. Though there is middle ground to be found, she disregards it and goes all or nothing. We need to help people think about why something happened and help them recognize that it isn't the end of the world. Indeed, something positive may have even come from it. Nothing in life is ever black and white; you need to search for the grey in the middle.

I'm guilty of this myself. I once said, "If a member of my team makes a mistake then it is ultimately my fault." While this is true to a degree because they follow my processes, I can't make all this a *personal responsibility*. A better way to approach this is to simply look at the mistake and ask yourself why it happened and how to avoid it in the future.

Similarly, if something has gone wrong we may *generalise*. I sometimes hear people say, "This always happens to me!" There are certain words in the English language that we need to be wary of, like never, every, and always. Have you ever said the following:

"I'm never doing that again!"

"I always hate dealing with that person!"

"Every time they come into the office something goes wrong."

Do these types of statements affect your future actions and interactions?

Take Care of your Mental Health

In some cases, the thinking traps I've noted can be signs of an adverse mental health issue. It can be especially important to notice if someone is constantly falling into thinking trap black holes, as this behaviour can be linked to mental health. I don't believe that enough is said about mental health for business owners. Anxiety and depression can be a major problem in business. People can struggle to cope and can have great challenges digging themselves out of trying situations. Thinking traps can be a sign that someone is experiencing difficulties.

Listen for thinking traps in conversations. It's worth catching people out and asking them exactly why they think (or speak) as they do. It can lead to some great conversations, though you might avoid suddenly saying, "Aha! You've used a thinking trap" and instead try a softer approach. Aim to be someone they can trust, someone they feel comfortable sharing with.

Research by the Association of Chartered Certified Accountants (ACCA) during the early part of the 2020 COVID pandemic revealed that 11% of business owners had considered suicide. That is a horrific statistic!

The Office for National Statistics (ONS) discovered that between 2011 - 2015 suicide was the leading cause of death for people under the age of 50. Furthermore, it showed that the higher prevalence of suicide was amongst males (80%). Sobering statistics. The findings of the ACCA and ONS suggest that the state of mental health amongst business owners is poor. When I hear a client say "I might jack it all in" it's a warning sign to me.

If I hear someone being caught up in despair with their business, I'll follow up a week later to make sure they're ok. They may be caught up in a thinking trap because something minor has gone wrong, but it's worth exploring further. Most thinking traps don't signal anything drastic. But it's still important to understand the truth underlying a thinking trap and then to work to combat that trap.

What can you do about a thinking trap?

There are a couple of things you can do to avoid thinking traps and to keep a check on your own mental health:

1. Identify when you or someone else is using a thinking trap. Merely acknowledging it will help you better understand situations and feel more in control.

2. Practice letting go of things. I try (not always successfully) to stop my brain from going down into a black hole. I read a hugely popular book called *The Chimp Paradox* by Steve Peters which gives a deeper understanding of how the brain works. The book is a great read for gaining a greater insight into the control you can exert on your own mind. Remember that your brain acts on emotion and emotions lead us to act impulsively. Our wonderful scientists have put people into brain scanning machines to prove that blood flows to these regions when we are upset or emotional. You need to recognise that your decisions can be impaired when you are angry or under pressure. You might not be able to fully let go of something but recognising your emotions can help you to manage stress better and to more effectively schedule important decisions. There have been some fascinating studies into mindfulness. Research by the University of Exeter showed that mindfulness is a good way for people recovering from depression to live a life without taking antidepressants. I've used mindfulness myself during periods of high stress and, though I have no scientific evidence for it, I felt it was easier to get to sleep and to let go of the things surging through my brain.

3. Sometimes doing nothing is best. I know that might be a strange thing to say but I've found that rushing to solve stressful problems can backfire. Allowing some time to pass can help some of that stress dissipate and allow you to make a more controlled

decision later on. I once had a terrible situation at work where I was angry with someone. My first instinct was to write an email threatening legal action. However, I left it for two months before I did anything about it. What I couldn't see initially was that person's objectives. As those two months passed, the other party couldn't handle the inaction and ultimately showed their hand. I've used this to great effect over the years and often told clients to simply leave things for a few days and see what happens.

What have I learned?

I have written about how I go about setting goals and forming habits. I'm a driven chap, yet I'm aware that being driven comes at a cost. I felt this was an important chapter at this stage of the book for exploring how we can acknowledge the words we choose and our overall state of mind. I'm often in the situation of being overwhelmed. I'm a father of two young children, a husband, a triathlete, a businessman, a part time lecturer at a university, an aspiring author, an e-learning content builder, and a man of many hopes and dreams.

Over the years I've become (maybe this is an age thing) comfortable with not being able to do everything. My priorities in life have changed and I have a better understanding of my own brain. I know that not being able to achieve everything can be a cause of stress, for me and for many other people.

Stress can be both a huge driver and disrupter in our lives, but with some carefully targeted study we can alleviate it. It's rare for me now to struggle with getting to sleep due to having an overactive mind. The worst thing you can do with stress is to not acknowledge it. Someone once told me, "Stress is relative. Even the cleaner will feel stress. We all just have different stresses."

You will have your own personal triggers that send you down into one of those black holes and cause stress. For me, I love triathlons. I love the training, I love the people, I love racing, and I love the trips away. But (and this is a big but!) my body sometimes has other ideas and it breaks down. I get injured. This can make me feel like part of my heart has been torn out. I say things like "this could be the end of my triathlon life" and "I'm going to be out for ages!" Thinking traps! Yet when I talk to people they say "Don't worry you'll get better in no time" or "Make sure to fully recover so you can enjoy some of your season" or "What did the medical professional have to say?" my whole perception of the situation changes for the better. If other people can reveal our thinking traps for us, we can do the same for ourselves through awareness and understanding.

9

The Art of Learning
The science of learning

I wrote earlier about learning French and mentioned my struggles with dyslexia. As a result of both, I've picked up a few things about learning a new skill.

It was the first year of the pandemic and my family and I were planning on holidaying in France, but it was cancelled. Instead, with only a week's notice, we were off to Italy. My years of studying French weren't going to be put to good use.

"I've wasted my time learning French," I lamented.

There's one of those darn thinking traps again!

I needed to direct my frustration. So being a competitive guy, I wondered if I could learn Italian in a week. When I started learning French I used an app called Duolingo. I was hooked on Duolingo because it works on the principle of streaks. For example, it kept track of how many days in a row I studied. At the time, I had a very lengthy streak of 450 days. Yes, I'd formed a habit, but this habit didn't feel healthy and it needed to be broken! I realised I wasn't making any real progress and that my level of French wasn't improving. I was merely addicted to continuing my streak. Yes, Duolingo was a good tool to get me started but I should've given up on it after six months. In hindsight, there may have been more effective ways of learning.

So how on earth was I going to learn Italian in one week?

I looked this time to science, and the Pareto principle (see Chapter 5) was the first thing I thought of. Of all the words that commonly get spoken in a language, 80% of them come from only 20% of that language's total number of words. So I printed off a sheet of the 2000 most used words in Italian. I didn't want to spend my time on words that rarely get spoken!

I also realised from my French studies that <u>80% of my learning was coming from only 20% of my study time</u>. When I considered some of the study tools I'd used in the past, I recognized that I'd been wasting time. Despite the considerable amount of time I spent using Duolingo, I was actually getting 80% of my knowledge from my much less frequent face to face tutoring lessons. The time I spent on my bad habit of chasing streaks on Duolingo could easily have been diverted to more efficient types of studying.

To learn Italian, this time I followed these key concepts:

1. *to be*, *to have*, *to make*, and *to take* are the most useful verbs in any language. For example, most Romance languages like Italian use the verb *to take* when ordering in restaurants. I decided to print off the present tense conjugations of these verbs. If I could nail those few verb conjugations, I would at least be able to make a passable effort at the language in common restaurant situations.

2. I found a list of the most used pleasantries, such as *thank you*, *no problem*, *excuse me*, and *sorry*. These simple yet extremely common words are very useful, and they get used every day. Think about interactions in a supermarket where you need to squeeze past someone and want to be polite - well, that's the very simple "Scusa!" Knowing this single word may not seem like much, but it actually helps a lot on many occasions.

3. I used an app, but not Duolingo this time. I used Memrise, which works on the principle of learning the most common words in a language. It repeats those words and tracks how often you get them correct. The basics of repetition are so important for my own language learning. Repetition tends to build long term memories by creating strong chemical interactions at the synapses of your neurons. If you're like me and you don't really understand that stuff, just remember that repetition works – science says so!

4. Learning can take place in many different ways. Depending on how your brain is wired, you will have particular learning styles that suit you best. I can tell you that I absorb information best with visual and kinesthetic teaching techniques. Regardless of your specific learning styles, which you may not know anyway, it's always best to incorporate lots of different types of learning into your routine. I listen to French radio while driving and I read a science website called Futura Science. I use phone apps, I take face to face lessons, and I write notes in French. I view youtube videos, I listen to podcasts, and I read novels. The technological world we live in means that it has never been easier to appeal to distinct learning styles. I hope you'll notice that I'm utilising all sorts of contrasting materials and methods to ensure my brain has access to all the best possible learning opportunities. I applied this same strategy to my week of learning Italian with great success.

5. Look for dead time and make it productive. I used Bluetooth to stream an Italian radio station and Italian podcast while I was driving. This turned my commute into a golden learning opportunity.

6. Use what you've learned about habit formation. I already had the habit of using language apps for 20 minutes in the evening. For my French studies, the apps have now been replaced with reading. Some people say you shouldn't study at bedtime, but find what works for you. My personal goal was to create the habit of reading in a foreign language for

pleasure, and now I do that in the evening. Overall, there hasn't been a single day where I haven't done something with my study of French.

The million-dollar question: Could I speak Italian by the time I went to Italy?

Of course I couldn't!

BUT! I could ask for basic things in a restaurant. I could comprehend certain words and signs. And I received compliments from Italians about how nice it was that I'd made an effort to speak in their language. Most importantly, it had taken me *months* of work to get to a similar point with French when I had been following the principle of total immersion.

Another exciting part of the week-long Italian challenge is that I've retained a number of Italian words. They are embedded in my brain because of repetition. When I compare my progress, I'd say that my one week of Italian study was equivalent to 6 weeks of French study.

I should note something about my study of Italian. A study conducted by the University of Haifa showed that it is easier to learn a third language when you have already gained a good understanding of a second language. Italian is also a romance language like French, so I had the benefit of understanding things like gender and number. However, I'm confident that my change in learning methods allowed me to grasp in one week more than I ever could have imagined.

So how can you apply this to your business?

If you need to learn something, search out the most effective way of doing it. The following tips are especially important if you are in charge of teaching something to a team of people.

Top tips:

- Don't presume you can teach everyone the same way. You need to appeal to different learning styles by utilising a wide variety of resources. The types of learning styles include visual, auditory, reading & writing, and kinesthetic. Go and do some research about these and other learning styles.

- There are some fun tests on the Internet which will tell you which learning style is best for you. But remember: just because it works for you doesn't mean it works for everyone. And keep in mind that you yourself can gain from learning in alternative ways. Though I know that I'm a kinetic learner, I try to build in all sorts of different materials and methods into my learning.

- Try to form one or two study habits and you'll reap the dividends. A small effort each day will help you. You can do the same for teams – provide them with routines that include conducive learning environments and consistent times for them to learn.

✻ I had to change careers and therefore had to learn new things very quickly. I can be given something to read, but I need to adapt this activity to my personal learning style. When I would look at tax legislation, I'd choose to use paper and a calculator to work stuff out for myself. And if I used an example from a real life situation it would cement the knowledge in my brain more effectively.

✻ I'm forever being asked by people, "How did you learn how to do that?" It's easy: I worked harder, I studied harder, and I used specific & focused study techniques. I'm not an academic genius, but I'm disciplined and focused.

Whatever you set out to accomplish or learn, take time to think before you launch into it. I'm always looking for new and inventive methods to teach things. I once launched a new business marketing campaign mere hours before going to teach at the university because I was in need of real data to show during the lecture. Lecturing can be difficult when you're trying to appeal to kinesthetic learners, so I always try to show real life examples that relate to the real world.

If learning is not part of your life but you want it to be, try learning an easy skill first. Build from there. Create even the smallest routine in your life and you'll get better at forming habits, including learning habits. Your first small learning habit will be a foundation for future habits. Clever things, habits!

10

Coaching & Mentoring
Being supported by others

I t will not surprise anyone who knows me that I'm a tad competitive. I quickly realised that being at the back of a triathlon race is no fun!

So I wanted to go faster, but how?

This chapter is about a fascinating area of science called "Human Performance Science." We tend to have a good understanding of what this means when it comes to sport. It's why my story starts with my challenges in sport and then continues with how this translates into a work setting. My objective is to explore the importance of a network and the impact of people who can act as mentors and coaches.

The Story of People

I realised after my first full triathlon season that I needed help. I went to Parkrun, swam at the triathlon club, and occasionally did a bike ride. I had pains in my legs that neither my GP nor the NHS physiotherapist could explain. I was exhausted after each race and it took me a whole week to recover.

The races I did that season were sprints, which perhaps don't sound too difficult. But when I speak of a "sprint," I refer to a 750m swim (usually in a cold lake), a 20km bike, and a 5km run. And I do all of it as fast and hard as I can. Honestly, this is what I do for fun! In hindsight, I realise that a triathlon sprint was a massive ask of my body and that it needs enormous respect. The word "sprint" is a trick! But how could lessons from business help with my triathlon problems?

In my business life, I get either a man or woman at the end of the phone who can more or less answer any of my questions – they are specialists in their field. After years of being in business, these people in my contact list are fantastic at what they do. They are at the top of their game. A network of skilled people I'd helped out, worked with, referred people to, or done the odd favour for.

I realised I could do the same with triathlon. I needed the best people to sort out my painful legs, so I asked around and found a physiotherapist named Neil. He diagnosed my leg problems in 4 minutes! Neil, a pleasant and mild-mannered chap, recommended a massage to fix my legs. A massage! Did he not know how painful these legs are?

Except this was no relaxing massage. It was the massage from Hell! He tortured me for 40 minutes on the massage bed (which I affectionately referred to as "the rack"). I'm surprised he'd not offered me a stick to bite down on to manage the pain.

"This is why appointments only last 45 minutes, as people can't hack an hour," Neil reassured me at the end of the appointment. He was right. It had been hell! And the next day it felt like someone had beaten my legs with a club. However, he cleared me for running, and five days later I ran a 10-mile race.

But the real magic happened at the very end of the massage appointment. He moved from a practitioner to a coach. He explained to me about the makeup of my body and how I should be using a foam roller for self myofascial release. He explained that this would help relieve muscle soreness, improve my joints' range of movement, and increase blood flow. He impressed upon me the need to stretch, especially if recovering from injury, and that I must seek professional advice if injured.

If a professional like Neil could give me this kind of advice verbally in five minutes, what other advice could I get if I had other people on hand?

So I asked around for a coach and was directed to Andy. People loved working with him. He'd coached amateur athletes through Iron Man triathlon events and even had some nationally ranked amateur athletes in his care.

I told him my biking wasn't very good, and we agreed he'd have a look at my Strava (an activity tracking app). I was super excited as there was loads of data for him to look at. I could only imagine what this man of so many years of experience would do with the data.

"I know what's wrong with your biking," Andy told me a few days later.

"You don't do enough! You're not doing the right type of training or enough of it. If you want to be a fit and healthy triathlete, you need structure. It's not just your biking. Did you know doing things like strength training helps with injury prevention?"

"But what about all the data!? What about that graph which tracks my fitness?" I said, feeling a bit hurt by his in-depth data analysis.

"Forget the data, Justin. The quality and type of the training are what matter. That data might be useful later."

Within a week, I had a structured training plan from a qualified professional who had studied human behavioural science. Thank goodness I found him because I'd never have known what to do. He provided me with honest feedback that no one else had offered. A coach is a person who sees the best and the worst. They know when to tell you the motivating stuff and the feedback you need to hear. Even if you don't always like hearing it! (I'm always telling clients things they don't want to hear, but I see myself as a similar type of coach and mentor for many of them.)

I now had a coach designing a weekly training plan for me and giving me feedback after each session. He spent a lot of time putting together a well planned training strategy, so I felt obligated to give it my best shot. It also helped having someone hold me accountable – it made me feel like I was letting him down if I didn't do my training. Being held accountable is a significant driving force for getting you off your backside. We often already know what we need to do, but we just aren't doing it.

Imagine for a moment you created a to-do list. Now add someone looking over your shoulder, guiding you as you accomplish things. Maybe making the odd suggestion about how you could do a task more effectively. And it's important to imagine them being pleased with your accomplishments, rather than being disappointed with anything. Do you think you'd get more done with this helpful assistant? Of course you would, and there's science to back that up. As humans, we are massively influenced by social pressure. Our brains have evolved over thousands of years to include a strong desire to "fit in." So if you are being held accountable you conform to this ingrained social pressure.

This theme of coaching continues with my current triathlon life. I work with a new physio who represented GB in the Olympics and works with a range of athletes. I had orthotics made for me by someone supporting another GB team. I have a chiropractor who keeps an eye on my spinal alignment. They all hold me accountable in some form or other. For example, I might be asked to do some stretching or strength exercises, and my physio uses a device to measure muscle force that will show if I haven't been doing the work. How great to see my physio using data and information! Although I better not make sarcastic jokes in case my coach ever reads this.

My coach and health professionals have been trained in their specialised areas. Yet they share an interesting common trait: they have studied and gained similar qualifications specific to human behavioural science. In addition to studying the body, training loads, and all that kind of thing, they have dedicated time to learn about the human behavioural science that can be utilised to guide and assist us.

Coaches and Mentors in Business

I've never paid for a business coach but over the years I've had lots of mentors around me. It doesn't have to be a formal relationship, but finding them is a good idea.

I have worked in accountability groups, which are a great way to set goals in a team environment and harness the power of social pressure. I've found accountability groups can give me outside opinions and new perspectives.

The brilliant mentors in my life have done all the things I'm writing about. They gave me deadlines to achieve goals, offered advice about something I've done, and suggested how it could be improved. They'll give me useful new perspectives and unbiased advice. And occasionally they'll even tell me that something I did was a new perspective for them and that they'd learned something from me.

So what to do if you want to work with a business coach?

There are formally recognised qualifications for business coaching but keep in mind that anyone can set up as a business coach. I can be slightly disparaging about paid business coaches. Sometimes a coach can cross into areas they don't understand and you need to tread carefully. It's important to understand the skills of any coach before you start. The problem with a good business coach is they are like rocking horse shit. It's very difficult to find a good one and a business owner needs to have the drive and determination to act on the advice.

It's necessary to remember that coaches and mentors can't do everything by themselves. Before you start considering if coaching will work for you, consider if you have the willpower to overcome some challenges. I highly encourage you to bring a level of motivation and open-mindedness to your efforts so you're able to take new ideas on board. After all, my triathlon coach can't make me do the training – I need that all important willpower. He simply applies tried and tested techniques that help nudge me in the right direction.

Different areas of the brain control our wills and won'ts. If we feel passionate about something, whether it's a business or triathlon, then you'll be able to access the "will" part of the brain.

If you think you have the determination to follow the advice of a coach, then go for it and commit to a financial relationship. Make sure to get recommendations, then ensure they have specific "pre-develop tools" and a plan they intend to have you follow. My triathlon coach doesn't aimlessly set me training sessions. I know he has different phases and pre-developed sessions that he implements based on which races I'm doing. It's the same in business. You need a coach who understands such phases and uses tactics that are deployed strategically from day one onwards.

There is a reason why ActionCOACH has become the world's biggest business coaching organisation. They have developed excellent processes, tools, techniques, and training. Yet even they understand the challenges: the website description of their 1-2-1 Program reads, "This program is not for the faint-of-heart nor the uncommitted."

If you don't think a coach is for you, then try to find a mentor or business colleague who can help you set goals and hold you accountable.

Goal setting will fire up different parts of your brain and the ideas will start flying, but be sure to know what your ultimate goals are. Stick with them, and ensure that your coach or mentor is in agreement about them.

I've said this before – to make money we can only do three things: raise prices, cut costs, or sell more. So where do these three factors sit in relation to the goals you set with a coach or mentor?

I have a client who spent £700 per month on a business coach over 18 months. Her business didn't perform any better during that time. You have to ask the question: what happened?

If I'm honest, the client didn't have the willpower or experience to act on some of the advice. The business coach should probably have assessed whether the relationship had value. That might sound a little harsh but if you can't get results, then the relationship isn't working. When I questioned the client, she said she was quite happy with the relationship because she had someone to talk to. This is where maybe coaching and mentoring have been mixed up. So what's the difference between the two?

The Power of a Great Mentor

While at university in 2003, I set up a business with a group of friends as part of our degree program. I was assigned a mentor by the university, a mentor who carried on in this capacity for many years.

How did we pick her?

The university organised a lecture so the mentors could introduce themselves. In walks Joanna, who promptly falls down the stairs. So that was a key criterion to us choosing her! She'll be horrified that I've put this in the book.

In all seriousness, my team was trying to start a business that would sell business cards in the form of small compact discs. Joanna had worked in London running her own PR & media small business, so she was a perfect fit.

After my university team disbanded, I continued to work with her. The only issue was that sometimes when she offered her worldly wisdom I just ignored it. We can all find a great coach or mentor, but we need to listen once in a while! One of the things she helped me with was improving my business English skills. I had never realised this was its own skill.

"Justin, your business English needs to improve if you're going to be a director!"

"Show me what I'm doing wrong!" I pleaded.
I was desperate to improve my English skills and had been working hard for many years. My goals were aligned with this advice and the willpower was there, so I jumped for joy at the opportunity. Though I struggled with dyslexia, I've never used it as an excuse. An excuse is just a statement about an unset goal in an area where one needs to improve. My competitors who don't have dyslexia don't care about it, so why let it hold me back?

As I worked hard on my English, Joanna could see my care and diligence and she continued to give me feedback. That's the great thing about a brilliant mentor – if they can see you doing the right thing they will be genuinely happy for you.

The other mentor who has been a great assistance is my mum, who ran her own firm of solicitors. She's a tenacious woman who can hold her own against anything. (On one occasion a fight broke out at reception. The receptionist ran right past the two male solicitors' offices to get my mum, a 5ft tall, slightly built woman.) She's a strong leader of people who showed great loyalty to her firm's staff. With her business partner, she grew a new business to four offices across the North East of England. She had respect amongst the other solicitors in the town, all the while being a single parent (who dragged me along to Law Society dinners) She's been a great source of business advice and legal knowledge. (More on my mum in my chapter "Down at the Police Station.") The actions of a mentor can sometimes be as powerful as the advice they give.

But a mentor doesn't have to be someone you know. I have lots of informal mentors, such as clients who work in all sorts of industries. They have become unexpected yet valuable mentors to us. A great skill we've acquired is to listen to them carefully. One client comes to mind, a chartered surveyor who now works at a senior level in a floated company. When he speaks about business problems in his job, I listen intently. I realise that I'm gaining and absorbing business knowledge from every word that comes out of his mouth.

It's a useful skill to identify what various people in a room can offer. When unexpected mentors can provide knowledge and experience, it's an efficient (and cheap) way to learn.

Who is coaching and mentoring you?

Part 3 Practical Applications of Practical Applications of Science

11

Building a Shed
Small changes, networks, and working on a business

A s scientists we need to stop once in a while to reflect.
It's part of the scientific process.

I've picked a few subjects which are critical to business
success for my third and last section of the book. I want to
help you bring together the ideas from the "Scientific
Principles" and "The Brain and People" sections. I'll give
you examples and stories about how they can be put into
action and hopefully show you the power they hold.

It's now time to start the process of reflection and to get a
glimpse of how I reflect and think deeply about various
concepts. This chapter is the perfect point to start some of
that reflection. My last chapter looked at coaches and
mentors so this chapter follows perfectly.

Marginal Gains

I've introduced numerous concepts so far and I've enjoyed telling you about my journey to become a triathlete. But the million dollar question is: did all the coaching, mentoring, analysis, nutrition, and changes make a difference? Hell yes!

After implementing everything during my next racing season, I smashed my personal bests and I finished in the top 30 in a couple of events. In 2021 I finished just outside the top 3% at the Great North Run half marathon.

If we look at all the things I've accomplished, the huge gains can't be attributed to just one thing. Taking on a coach showed me what could be achieved if I embraced his knowledge of sports science. Things like conditioning training, structured interval sessions, pre-race builds, training phases, increasing the volume, and quality of training. They all contributed. My coach was a conductor and all those things were the separate movements that combined to create a beautiful symphony.

Aside from listening to my coach, I undertook my own research to become familiar with the concepts and theories of sports scientists and nutritionists. I developed a personal nutrition strategy and I used data from my own training; I tracked, I measured, and I improved. Basically, I started to think smarter. It's fascinating when you start to do this. The Olympic triathlete Jonny Brownlee, of whom I'm a big fan, once said that as he's gotten older he's had to get smarter about the way he trains. I figure he's a good person to listen to!

I've long been figuring out how to "get smarter." That tasty beetroot juice was just something small, but it was a beginning. Following on from that was my foam roller, then each element my coach introduced, then finding a physio, analysing data, looking at nutrition, etc. It isn't a fluke that all these small factors added up to a bigger sum. This is the concept of marginal gains.

Keep that in mind as I share something which is important to how we go about changes. I came across a philosophy from the world of cycling that was developed by David Brailsford, the Director of Sport for the professional cycling outfit TEAM INEOS (formerly TEAM SKY). It's an innovation initiative that's all about marginal gains. With the crackdown on illegal drug usage in pro-cycling, pro teams suddenly had money to spend on innovation. This is no joke – a third of their budgets had been going towards performance enhancing drugs!

Brailsford's TEAM SKY implemented a strategy of searching out every little thing they could to add small marginal gains. Michael Hutchinson chronicled this in his 2014 book about cycling, *Faster*. Hutchinson followed the GB cycling team during its attempts to get faster. In the book he describes all the small changes that the team made. (By the way, Michael's book is where I've pinched that comment about a third of the budget being used on drugs.)

I realised I'd stumbled on pure business gold! Marginal gains…from a book about cycling! There are people who are critical of marginal gains but the GB cycling team's world-beating success is a great example of what such a philosophy can achieve.

Pure science does not always give rise to innovation change. Innovation is often driven by human inventiveness, and TEAM INEOS' quest for speed is a great case in point.

Running a business is much the same. No single thing made me a better triathlete or improved my business, and no single thing will do the same for you. But if you search for as many opportunities and small adjustments as possible, you'll find they'll all add up.

Creating a Network

Building a network of people is invaluable especially when it comes to looking for marginal gains. In the last few chapters I've talked about having people around me and that's called having a network. As my business career has developed over time, networking has changed. But let me start at the beginning.

At the age of 22 I set up a business. After a few weeks I noticed something. The phone wasn't ringing! The idea of marketing came to mind (more on that shortly) so we printed car stickers and pens, sent out letters, and placed a yellow pages ad (remember those!?). Guess what! The phone still wasn't ringing. We needed customers!

I picked up the phone to my mum. "How do I get clients?"

"I'll give you Gus's phone number," she replied.

"Doesn't Gus own a building company!?"

I was a bit bemused – I thought she was going to tell me how to get clients, not to speak to a builder!

"Ah yes, but he knows everyone, and I bet he has some suggestions for what you're trying to do," my mum explained.

So I rang Gus in the hope he might feel sorry for me and give me some work. He didn't give me any work, but he did something even more important - he started me on a journey. I didn't know it then but he was the first person in my new network.

Gus spent 20 minutes with me on the phone for no other reason than I was Catherine's son. The outcome of the conversation was him giving me the number of someone else. He told me that person had joined a structured networking group that would probably be good for me, too. That subsequent conversation led me to join a networking group called BNI (Business Network International). I ended up being a member for almost 10 years.

At first, however, I checked out BNI and was pitched with the cost: £500 plus £6 a week for breakfast! My god, I don't have that sort of money! Don't you know I need more clients? But I took a risk and put the payment on a credit card, and it was the best money I ever spent.

I didn't know anyone when I first set up my business, but BNI provided structured networking. It's not everyone's cup of tea but it was exactly what I needed. The groups are run by volunteers and as soon as I had the chance I became the membership coordinator, the role with the largest amount of admin. So why did I choose to do that?

Because I wanted to be seen. I wanted to prove myself and, most of all, I wanted everyone who joined to know my name and to see I was capable. It's amazing what being in a position of authority can do. (More on this science in my chapter "Hi, I'm Dan.").

Becoming the membership coordinator worked like a charm. I did everything (with a smile!) including member recruitment and the dreaded cold calling. It took me a year to build up close relationships with people but I still have many of the same names in my contact book to this day. Some even followed me as I switched from one career to another. They didn't care that "Website Justin" had become "Accountant Justin."

(They had bought into the Justin brand. The Justin brand? Really? Well yes! It was a brand that stood for honesty, ethics, and integrity. It represented someone who was supportive, kind, and a great listener. Someone who would give his support not to gain something for himself but simply to give to others.)

As my 10 years with BNI went by, children came along and getting up at 6am was no longer practical. Plus I felt that I'd outgrown BNI. My networking had taken a new form that mainly consisted of my existing close connections. I was also finding it frustrating that some of the new members joining the group were not complimenting my existing network.

There's a scientific theory called "Dunbar's number" that says a human being can only maintain 150 meaningful relationships. I was realising that once I had a top-notch person in my contact book, I was finding it hard to create a meaningful relationship with anyone else from the same field. (Check out the concept of mastermind groups for more on this idea.) I recognised that, somewhat by accident, I'd created my own network that was difficult to improve upon or increase in size. My networking had moved to a new phase where I was more interested in strengthening the relationships I already had. I was educating myself about the people I already knew so that I could have better relationships with them in the future.

Another science-related principle that relates to networking is "six degrees of separation." You've probably heard of it. It began with an interesting study carried out in 1929, and the principle is still valid. The premise holds that you are never more than six people away from anyone else in the world. Though the world's growth in population size since 1929 might suggest this is no longer true, new communication technologies may have actually reduced our distance from other people to fewer than six connections!

Let's take the current Prime Minister. I worked out that I may be as few as three or four people away from communicating with the PM. I realised that (1) someone I went to school with has a (2) family member who works in Downing Street, so he would have direct contact with the (3) PM or at least with (4) someone who works with the PM. It took some technology and a good bit of cyber sleuthing to discover the connection, but there it was.

The business social networking site LinkedIn works on this principle. It works great, though we can do the same without such a formal structure. I can rely on the principles of "six degrees of separation" and "Dunbar's number." If I have my 150 connections and then take advantage of those people's 150 connections, I'll have a network of 22,500 people at my fingertips.

The next step is to become an expert in your own field. When someone has a problem, you want them to think about YOU. The moment one of your clients or friends has a problem and needs to employ specialised services, you want your name to be the first one out of the hat. And once they've contacted you, their problems are opportunities for you to help freely, to *give* something. A principle of BNI is the concept of Givers Gain. If you give someone some business, they'll want to pay it back to you. Scientists have determined that it is the givers in business who have the best long term prospects. Studies also show that you'll likely feel much happier when you give. I try all the time to go out of my way to help someone. It's not something I force myself to do but something I *want* to do. I feel great when I share some of my expert knowledge.

Let me briefly relate this discussion of networking to that of marginal gains. If we take each one of our contacts as a stand-alone, they might not have much of an effect. But each person is a marginal gain that increases the pool of skills and knowledge.

Really spend some time learning about networking as it's one the most powerful tools in your arsenal.

How to work on your business

Now you understand the concept of marginal gains, you understand the power of networks, and you see how coaches can help. And you have ideas...but next you need to implement them. There's a modern buzz phrase I often hear: "working on your business." I hate this phrase because I don't think people have any idea what "working on your business" means. I believe it's about the deliberate application of proven theories and tools. If you're just guessing at what "working on your business" means, you might not see the results you desire.

Let me tell you about Paul, one of my clients.
"I'm going to employ somebody so they can do the day-to-day stuff and I'm going to do other work on my business. Hopefully, this will result in some growth and I'll end up taking on more staff," Paul declared.

"Great, let's follow up in a few months," I replied.

A few months later, Paul returned to my office.

"How has it been going?" I asked.

"After a couple of days of writing facebook posts, I realised I've got no idea about how to work on my business. So I've mainly enjoyed the nice weather in the garden," Paul admitted.

He told me that his new employee had been doing the day to day work. However, the business wasn't growing. Paul explained that he was going to let the employee go and he would go back to doing the day to day work. It's unfortunate – Paul simply wasn't implementing the right things or doing so in the most effective way.

This is not an uncommon story. Another client recently told me about what he does when he doesn't have any work to do. He's a one-man operation that does specialised motor parts repair. He proudly told me that when business has been slow, he's been building a shed in his garden.

"How does your employer feel about that?" I cheekily inquired.

"But…I'm my own boss," he replied with a worried look on his face.

"Brilliant! I presume building a shed is helping with your sales and marketing? Or with your process documents? I did notice your bookkeeping hasn't been kept up to date…"

"Ok I get the point!"

I had some pertinent follow-up questions.

"Would you like to earn more money?"

"Absolutely! My girlfriend wants us to buy a house together."

"Then forget building sheds for a little while and write me a list of all the things you need to do. Even if you don't know how to do them yourself."

I spoke to him about networking and how to build contacts. I explained how he could engage with his local motorsport community and position himself as an expert.

"What about providing some free mechanical support at race meetings? Perhaps you could give them a leaflet. I'm sure you'll get something back later," I suggested. My message was clear. He needed to work on his business properly, trying things that had been proven to work.

I can't tell you absolutely everything you need to do to "work on your business" but my hope is that each chapter in this book is sharing things that worked for me in my business. Things that could work for you. By the way, my day job is working on people's taxes, but this book doesn't make any mention of it. (Thank goodness for that!) What I'm saying is that while I have to accomplish the day-to-day of my tax and accountancy job, I use other time to further develop the business. This might be writing processes, networking, creating newsletters, writing a book, etc. You might not have a lot of that extra time, but remember that 80% of business growth will come from 20% of your activities. Keep your focus on what is important. Marginal gains can be quick and easy fixes which add up. Look to add people to your network who can provide skills you might not have. Look for mentors or a coach who can help.

12

Increase Productivity by 30%
Embrace the knowledge behind innovation

I said in my last chapter marginal gains are an innovation initiative. But what exactly is innovation?

If we are going to work on our businesses, time needs to be allocated to innovation. "Working on your business" is actually the act of innovating. It happens every time we introduce something new. Any change, problem resolution, or opportunity being exploited is an innovation.

I was attracted to the study of innovation after I read about Google implementing something called "20% time." This was where workers could spend 20% of their work hours on any project they thought might benefit Google. One of the most notable projects to come out of this was Gmail.

The lesson from Google is you can't move your business forward unless you spend time developing and innovating.

It's fundamentally why I've always got some form of project on the go.

I've always loved creating new processes and products for our business. I'm like many entrepreneurs – prepared to take a few risks. What I've learned is that I can reduce the risks and put steps in place to increase the chance of success.

Success stems from realising that innovation is always happening in our businesses. Yet we sometimes don't recognise it, or we don't understand the science behind it.

I've been fortunate to teach innovation as one of the modules of a degree apprenticeship program. The participants are generally from a professional background and working for large organisations, and I taught them how academic knowledge feeds into innovation.

One memorable module group consisted of members of a regional police force. Despite the police force being a large organisation not normally conducive to change, the participants in this program module successfully delivered innovative change. One such change involved completing paperwork in a new way that increased the ease with which the Crown Prosecution Service (CPS) could push cases forward. Yes, even filling out some paperwork more intuitively is an example of innovation. The participants were able to change something and create a new method. It proved to me that when you embrace innovation you can make significant improvements, even in a complex organisation.

A case study from a different police force, Kent Police, helped us illustrate a point in the module. The case study involves a software product called Idea Drop. This innovative software allows any member of staff in the force to suggest an idea for consideration by senior leadership. Kent Police had a problem: it issued mobile phones to its officers, but the officers found that the phones were running out of charge by the end of shift. The people in charge didn't know about the problem, but a police officer used Idea Drop to share the problem. The key takeaway here is that the innovation of Idea Drop needed to exist in order for senior management to be aware of a problem. Management simply didn't realise there was a problem with mobile phone battery life, but Idea Drop connected them to someone in their own organisation who did. By the way, I've worked for one of the regional forces in the North East and know just how challenging it is to make technology changes in police cars. Idea Drop may seem like a simple concept but it served a very important purpose.

You might be interested in Idea Drop for your business, but keep in mind it's designed for bigger organisations. As an alternative, I managed to build my own innovation tool using a Trello board. (Trello is an online project management tool.) Even if your business isn't large enough for a major software tool, there are always ways to make effective changes and solve problems.

The Kent Police case study is a great example of a common problem: big organisations can be oblivious to problems due to limited communication between management and staff. Many large organisations have been caught napping when highly disruptive, competing businesses come along. AirBnB completely disrupted the B&B and hotel marketplace, very likely because that marketplace had been ignoring innovation.

I've encouraged innovation at everything from a nuclear power plant, a multinational pharmaceutical company, the NHS, a fish and chip shop, and a financial advising firm. Take the fish and chip shop. They decided to use a different type of sauce dispenser nozzle in order to reduce waste, while using the resulting time savings and reduced product cost to fund the purchase of recyclable containers. That's a marginal gain, and that's innovation. Sexy or exciting? Maybe not, but it was an effective innovation.

All the businesses I worked with had distinct innovation problems to be solved, but how I approached each of those unique problems was more or less the same.

So where do you start?

Think about innovations in terms of the 4Ps. All innovations fall into the following categories:

- Product: changes to your product or service
- Process: changes to the process you use to deliver your product or service
- Position: where you place your product in the market
- Paradigm (the overall business model): how you can change your overall model

Within these categories, your innovation will either be:

- Incremental (a small change), usually low risk / low cost / short development time
- Radical (a huge change), usually high risk / high cost / long development time

When James Dyson came up with the idea for a bagless vacuum cleaner, that was a radical change. It was a huge change to the market. It came with high risk, a high development cost, and a long project duration. On the other hand, deciding to add a lid to a previously lid-less ballpoint pen would reflect an incremental change to the product. Relatively easy to do and relatively low cost.

I want you to keep the 4P model in mind when you are making a change to your business. How does your change fit in the 4Ps? Are you going to be making a radical or incremental change? Let me show you an example...

How do we increase staff productivity by 30%?

Impossible! Before you think I'm joking, I'm not! Because this is an easy innovation problem to solve. I posed the question to my innovation students and got these answers:

- Ban talking
- Shorten lunch breaks
- Create a financial incentive program (Do you remember how this turns out?)
- Send them on specialist training

What would your solution be?

Mine was this: Give each staff member a second monitor! The cost of monitors for office work is relatively low, and most computers come pre-manufactured with an extra monitor port on the back so it's easy to add a second monitor. Researchers at Microsoft found that staff productivity increased between 9% to 50% when a second monitor was available. When you walk into my office, you see that every desk has two monitors. If you work in a finance field, two monitors will get certain tasks done in half the time!

When I consider the answers my students came up with, I am reminded of barriers and enablers. These are terms common when talking about innovation. My students' ideas were full of barriers – could you imagine your employer telling you that talking in the office was banned?! The second monitor solution has fewer barriers and more enablers.

By the way, if you're wondering under which of the 4Ps the monitor solution falls, it's Process. By adding more monitors, we were changing the way we delivered our service. And it was an incremental change because it was low cost and easy to apply.

Defining your problem

While teaching at Northumbria University, I was introduced to an innovation model called ADAPT (analysis, decision making, active risk taking, planning, and transition). The ADAPT model was developed by Richard Hale and Peter Whitlam.

I'm going to focus on the analysis part of ADAPT. If we can be better at analysing we can be more successful when we make changes to our business. When I work with business owners I see so many failures with new products or services during their initial development stages. Sometimes even the entire business fails. The analysis part of ADAPT is a simple technique that can help you avoid failure by giving your business a template for better understanding the problems that are requiring you to make changes.

Let's use my staff productivity 30% challenge as an example. What if my students had looked at it using something like a problem formulation grid:

	The problem is	The problem is not
What	To increase staff productivity	A lack of knowledge in the team
Where	Staff in the office and working at home	Facilities staff like cleaners and groundskeepers doing manual work
When	Certain tasks seem to be taking longer than other when working on certain software products	That we don't have good quality IT infrastructure.
How	Staff complain it takes them a long time to do certain tasks	When we are dealing with clients face to face during meetings
Who	Administrative staff Financial staff	Management Facilities management

Fig. 1 An example we use in our teaching at Northumbria University.

This simple grid allows us to pinpoint what the important problems are and, just as importantly, which things are *not* the problems. Furthermore, using this grid usually reveals the most crucial concerns. In this case, two key concerns are revealed: 1. The staff are complaining about particular tasks and 2. The most troublesome delays take place when the staff are using particular software products. But only by going through an established process of asking the right questions do we discover the most pressing problems. Notice that we don't have definitive solutions yet, but we're well on our way because we've pinpointed the actual concerns…and determined the things we don't need to worry about.

Perspectives

Finding potential solutions to the 30% productivity problem needs a further step once the analysis has been done. This next step involves the perspectives of people that will be affected by solutions. These people are referred to as the stakeholders. Part of the reason that my students' solutions to increasing productivity didn't work is that the students hadn't thought about the perspectives of all stakeholders. A potential innovation solution is often revealed as lacking once all the stakeholders' perspectives have been considered.

It's necessary to ask questions such as:

- How do staff members perceive the problem of productivity?
- How does management perceive it?
- How do our clients perceive it?
- How do shareholders perceive the problem?

Jawbone UP is a great example of a product that failed because all perspectives weren't considered. It was one of the first fitness trackers to the market, in 2011. By the end of 2011 they had secured $159m in funding. Apple even stocked the product in their stores. Most of their competitors didn't hit the market until 2012. But by 2016 they stopped production and they entered liquidation in 2017. So what went wrong?

They didn't pay attention to the perspectives of *all* of their stakeholders. And their customers made up a very important group of stakeholders whose needs weren't met. Jawbone UP didn't keep up with what their competitors were doing. Their design was groundbreaking but too much emphasis was being put on the design side of things rather than on gathering user data.

My point is this: gaining *all* perspectives gives you a much better chance of implementing a successful innovation.

I think this quote summarises it completely:

> **If I had asked the public what they wanted, they would have said a faster horse.**
> Henry Ford, founder of the Ford Motor company

If we imagine that Henry Ford had asked that question of his customer stakeholders, Ford would have heard that they wanted a faster horse. But, what's important is that he would have been able to pinpoint that what they actually wanted was *faster*. That word would have given the clue to what was truly needed from an innovation point of view.

There's one final step we now all need to consider. One of the areas we are all going to have to work on is how any business innovation impacts the environment. The better we understand the process of innovation, the better equipped we are to be equitable in our endeavours.

Responsible Innovation

Responsible innovation combines the considerations of people, planet, and profit. It involves finding a sweet spot among all these factors, not just with the environment.

In 2018 the second largest contributor to the World Health Organisation (WHO) was the Bill & Melinda Gates Foundation. Bill Gates made his fortune from Microsoft and has redirected billions of dollars into the pursuit of being equitable. It's quite an interesting innovation story.

There is a fascinating Netflix documentary called *Inside Bill's Brain*. It chronicles some of the fantastic projects undertaken by The Bill and Melinda Gates Foundation. The foundation's enormous pot of money aids them in their goal to help people live healthy, productive lives. The documentary focuses on three topics: improving sewage treatment in developing countries, the attempt to eradicate polio globally, and the development of clean energy from nuclear sources. The foundation spent over $200M alone on reinventing a toilet for the developing world! The documentary illustrates a shining example of what can be achieved when our only focus is being responsible...and when we throw any consideration of profit out of the window.

But most of us aren't Bill and Melinda Gates, so as typical business owners we are required to find a balance between profit and responsibility. Here's an example, and as you might expect, I ran it by my students first.

"How do you sell more toothpaste?" I asked them.

After 10 minutes thinking about the issue, they presented me with ideas such as rebranding/new packaging, making TV commercials, and giving out free samples.

I shook my head in disappointment and declared, "I'm a big multinational who only cares about profit so let's make the hole 1mm larger. It will result in 15-20% more toothpaste being used. It's a product change at an incremental level so why not do it?"

Of course, this is just a bit of fun. Surely we won't go down this route?

The problem is that humans, as innovators, have been doing just that – going down the wrong route! Rachel Carson's 1962 book *Silent Spring* was an early warning to the farming community that the choice to use chemical intervention in fields was the wrong one. The book led to the banning of DDT pesticides. However, the bigger message from the book was missed. While the book led to the banning of DDT, it didn't stop farmers from continuing to use many other harmful chemicals, and all in the name of innovation.

But there is hope.

In 1974 two scientists published arguably one of the most important scientific journal articles of our time. They joined forces with another scientist to effectively save the planet. Their work was so important it won them the Nobel Prize for Chemistry in 1995. Their names are Paul Crutzen, Sherwood Rowland, and Mario Molina. Their 1974 *Nature* magazine article identified the damage being caused by CFC gases to the Earth's ozone layer. Within four years countries had started banning the use of CFC gases, and in 1987 the Montreal Protocol established an agreement among nations to completely stop their use. Fast forward to today and we've seen a recovery in the Ozone layer which is being heralded as a (temporary?) saviour because it's slowing global warming. Maybe it's even giving us time to find a permanent solution to our warming planet.

Innovation created CFC gases, but innovation also saved us from them. When good science comes to the forefront we can innovate and undo our mistakes. Stop and ask yourself is there a more responsible way we can innovate before taking an idea forward to implementation.

A final word

Throughout the book so far I've mentioned many fundamental concepts, such as Occam's razor, marginal gains, and perspectives. All the concepts and subjects feed into practical innovation. For example, Occam's razor helps us find simple solutions, marginal gains are incremental innovations that are easy to implement, and perspectives enable truly effective solutions.

If you want to become a truly innovative business, you'll need one further thing to bring it all together. **Culture** is the innovation "glue" for any organisation. You need to address how you work with your people in order to be truly successful with innovation. Don't worry there is more to come on teams later in the book in the chapter called "The Importance of Work" Keep in mind some of these ideas from innovation when you start to think about getting a team to work effectively.

13

Going Green
How to save money and help the planet

This chapter has many of the components from innovation, Occam, data analysis, marginal gains, and 80/20. It also builds on innovation.

It's about a project where I made some mistakes, so it's the perfect place to reflect and learn from such errors.

We recently went through an exercise of counting carbon in our business.

Why?

Because it's coming! The need to report on carbon in your business is inevitable, so why leave it until the last moment? Plus, doing something about it now might save money.

I can tell you that as a business we produce 1,869kg of Co2e per head. I can also tell you our hybrid working style saves 2,100 commuting miles per annum, per member of staff. This equates to a saving of 370kg of Co2e per employee. Co2e is the combination of all the greenhouse gases such as methane, Co2, and nitrous oxide.

To get these numbers I had to collect loads of data from energy bills, commuting miles, types of cars used, water usage, and how much rubbish we produce. Then, with the help of an energy consultant, we turned the data into information.

The report's data was graphed, and one of these graphs clearly showed that commuting was generating 50% of our emissions. See below:

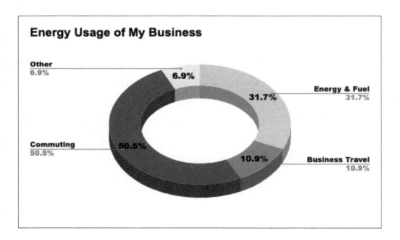

Yet when we added energy & fuels to commuting we found that familiar 80/20 split. Travel, heat, and power are essentially about 80%.

There were loads of other graphs and stats which were helping but they all came back to the measurement of kg of CO_2e. Not exactly the most useful unit of measurement, as I have no context for it. I can't visualise what kg of CO_2e looks like.

The relationship between energy usage and money is an easier concept to relate to and understand. So I started thinking about energy consumption…and the search for science began. One initial problem was that I'd already started a project of reducing my own energy consumption at home, long before I started looking for the applicable science. I'd been on the eco path for quite a number of years. I own an electric car and a smart water tank, I've got a flexible green energy tariff, I use solar panels with an energy storage battery, I have a solar diverter, and I've swapped many of our home products for greener alternatives.

When I found the science, I realised I'd done things in the wrong order! The issue is that I'd been taking the approach of "Fire, Aim, Ready" rather than "Ready, Aim, Fire." I'd not considered my problem correctly, which is a bit embarrassing considering I taught innovation! Because everything had been *home* projects, instead of being related to business, I didn't use any of the tools I'm describing in this book. Perhaps there's something to learn here about human nature!

The Search for Science

So how did I go wrong? When I decided I was going to improve my eco credentials, the first thing I bought was an electric car. But I was too focused on the shiny piece of metal, the gadget. In 2020, Direct Line Insurance did a comprehensive review of electric car savings from a monetary perspective and it came out as only 3%. (I do think this percentage has improved since the increases in fuel prices, and the study didn't look at flexible energy tariffs, but the review still made its point.)

After seeing this I realised I'd been a very silly boy. So I went looking for proper scientific studies, not just a review prepared by one company. I found a 2019 Eurostat study that showed nearly 80% of energy use is heating and hot water. (The 80/20 rule would appear to apply to energy in a wider setting.) Lighting and appliances come in second place at 14.1%. After reading the study and looking at my own home, I can also tell you that 80% of my appliance energy is consumed by only 20% of my appliances. (The main culprit is my clothes dryer!)

The mistake I initially made on my eco path was not undertaking the detailed defining of my innovation problems, as we saw in the problem specification grid section. What I should have done is analysed my own energy expenditures using those important data analysis techniques. If I reduce my monetary spend on energy, then of course Co2e will decrease.

Though the Eurostat study did not look at the use of transport, it made me think of doing so, and I found I was only doing 20,000 miles per annum. Yet I was spending £310 per month on gas and electricity costs in my home. Too much! And speaking of energy inefficiencies, my house, stone built and constructed over several decades in the 1700s and 1800s, is not exactly what you call energy efficient. So what did I do to improve my energy efficiency at home?

I should start by saying it can be so easy to find a solution to something even when we haven't stopped to analyse it. I fell into this trap! Though I have now achieved what I set out to do, I wish I'd applied some better analytical thinking from the beginning. Here are some examples of how proper analysis led to effective changes:

- When I saw how much energy my dryer was using, I immediately replaced it.

- I'd always taken the view that my heating and hot water system would be too tricky to tackle. I have a standard gas heating system like many homes and I couldn't easily switch to an alternative energy source. Nevertheless, I started some detailed analysis of my home energy so I could start to consider my options. Sure enough I discovered findings, similar to the EU study, that heating and hot water should be my primary targets, as they made up over 80% of my total energy usage. Though I wasn't expecting to find a simple solution, I began searching for studies that related to home heating. Without too much difficulty I came across a couple of studies. The first was from the UK Government, which investigated current heating controls such as thermostatic radiator valves and thermostats. This study showed that these basic (unintelligent) systems could potentially save money but there was very little robust data to say they worked well. For example, the study showed that the mean annual average home temperature was only 0.17°C lower if thermostatic radiator valves were used. Fairly poor! And here I was thinking I had standard controls in my house that were saving me lots of money.

The next study was an American research paper looking at the effectiveness of smart heating controls. I couldn't believe it – the savings were incredible. I'd dismissed these in the past as being too expensive yet the research was telling me I could repay the investment in just one year. When you compare this to my home solar energy system, which is 12 years to repay, it was mind blowing.

Here's an illustration of the advantage of using smart heating controls in my workplace:

I noticed that the heating was out of control in our office and the team were opening the windows in the middle of winter. A few years prior I'd fitted something called a zone value and two basic thermostats but we still couldn't control our top floor office. I'd spent £350-£500 doing this work and it had made little difference to the bill. Seems like that research of only saving 0.17°C and the lack of robust data with basic controls was indeed true. So I decided to implement smart thermostatic radiator valves. They were £70 each! Despite this, I took the plunge and the difference it has made is incredible. Rather than the room reaching 26 degrees, it is holding the room steady at 22 degrees. The first month of using this system I saved

17.1% of my energy. In monetary terms, that's about a £30 per month savings! I had the same experience at home after I implemented the system there.

There is actually some complex mathematics behind the scenes to consider heat control in buildings. But, if you're like me and you can't turn a simultaneous equation into an algebraic expression, then we need to turn to technology to provide the solution. That solution is having heat in a room reach the perfect temperature then having a software system turn off the thermostat automatically.

By the way, remember how I wrote that 80% of my energy consumption is heating and hot water? So what about the hot water portion? I came across a relatively new company in which two PhD researchers had come up with a different way to heat hot water. Rather than trying to heat the whole tank from the bottom up, they heated from the top down, and they only heated the amount that was needed. In effect, they took advantage of the scientific principle that hot water will float on top of cold water. Genius! Yet this wasn't good enough for the company. They also created an algorithm that determined *when* you would need hot water, therefore only heating the proportion of water you required at particular times.

On top of everything else, the tank has a solar switch to capture spare solar energy. This is what is called storing energy as potential energy. In fact, storing energy in hot water (provided the tank is well insulated) can be cheaper and more effective than an energy storage battery. These tanks can also communicate with the grid to pick up surplus energy, and they work as a network of tanks to help save energy on a national level. I remember learning about potential energy in school and it never really jelled in my mind. However, with the advent of green technology, you can see how this physics is so useful. Storing energy in batteries is just the storage of potential energy and the same science applies to the storage of energy in hot water. I've seen hydro plants pumping water to the top of a mountain when there is surplus energy so they can potentially store that energy. They then course it down the mountain when they need to generate electricity.

So, I installed one of these tanks and was blown away by the results. I benefited from intelligent water heating, national cooperation, a better-insulated tank, and being able to capture my spare solar energy. Unfortunately, I didn't realise I needed another piece of technology called a solar diverter, which is the "brain" that detects when I have spare solar energy. The diverter can choose what to do with energy based on the energy needs of the home. For example, if my solar battery is full then it heats water in the tank for later use. The diverter is great, though it was a £500 expense which I'd not expected.

The extra cost of the solar diverter was unfortunate but it has enabled me to explore installing a smart electric car charger. When my solar battery and water tank are fully charged then it charges the car with spare electricity. Let me put that a different way: imagine going to the petrol station and not paying for your fuel. Free fuel!

I do think the mistakes I made with the solar diverter reflected how I couldn't find experienced people to help me, so I was struggling to wrap my head around complex technologies. I was fortunate that I had already implemented a solar panel system, as it opened up possibilities for being innovative with the way I manage energy. The solar system is brilliant, but it's going to take several years to repay the capital outlay. The smart heating controls and water tank system were better decisions, as they're going to be repaid in one and four years, respectively. <u>So if you want to go green, target your heating and hot water first.</u> Don't make the mistake of rushing out to get that shiny new electric car just because it'll look nice on the driveway.

But what happens if you can't afford all these wonderful bits of technology? Well, Octopus Energy ran an interesting initiative that ran from December 2021 through February 2022 called the "Winter Workout." It was an exercise to illustrate that if people followed a series of tips requiring little or no expenditure they could reduce their energy consumption. I followed eleven of their tips and reduced my gas consumption by 15%, and I did see a drop in my bill. In fact, 118,408 Octopus customers saved over 5% in costs, which totalled £4.7M of savings.

Imagine if we could follow similar habits in our own lives and businesses. Savings can be reaped by making simple adjustments, which goes back to that theory of marginal gains. All the solutions Octopus suggested were simple, which keeps true to our friend Occam. It would be interesting to see how many Octopus tips people continue to use in the future. Maybe Octopus didn't realise it, but they were trying to train people to form new habits – habits which create small shifts that endure.

The Hard Data

I mentioned that I have an old house built before modern insulation, so I have few options to insulate my solid stone walls. There is around 300sqm of floor space so as you can imagine it has been a challenging project to reduce my energy consumption. I'll use it here as a good case study of what can be done in a business where spaces are larger and bills tend to be higher.

As always, I encourage you to start exploring data, so let's have a quick look at my own solar energy output from 2021. I generated 4,380 kilowatt hours (kWh) of electricity from my solar panels but only managed to use 2,719kWh. (So that means I gave away 1,661kWh to the National Grid!) However, my overall total energy consumption was 6,275kWh, which meant that I'd managed to get 43.3% of my total energy used from the sun. As you can see, the potential exists to increase that by 26.4%, if I can take advantage of that 1,661kWh of surplus energy I was unable to consume. If I can, it'll mean a saving of £250 per year.

Before I show you how much I've saved from a monetary perspective, I should mention another clever option I found. I discovered you can sign up for a flexible energy tariff. One of my suppliers told me how wind turbines continue to turn in the middle of the night, which results in a surplus of energy in the national grid that is sold at a discount. Between 12:30am and 04:30am, I can use as much as I like for only 5p per kWh. So this is when I charge my electric car and my solar battery. Furthermore, I buy this cheap energy and store it so that I can use it later, especially during the winter and early spring months. I've even programmed my water tank's onboard computer to know when it can activate the electricity to start heating.

Here are the stats on my yearly savings:

Around £410 via solar panels
Around £400 from the smart heating controls
£500 from my water tank
£48 charging my solar battery when energy is cheap overnight
£500 charging my car battery overnight

Total savings of £1,858

If we disregard the capital cost of my electric car, I spent about £14,000 changing and implementing eco-products in my house. If we take the saving of £1,858 and divide it by the capital outlay then you can calculate your return on investment. In this case it represents a 13.27% return on investment. As energy costs rise in the future my return on investment will increase as the savings will be greater.

So I've talked about smart heating control, water tanks, and solar and flexible energy, but what does it mean for saving energy?

I want to raise two points:

- I find it amazing that I've managed to save £1,858 per annum by changing my house to an eco house. Why can't we do this in our businesses? My smart heating controls, for example, have made a huge difference. That said, it's worth bearing in mind that smart heating controls give the fastest payback. The flexible energy tariff costs nothing to implement, but you need the infrastructure to take advantage of it. Solar panels are expensive and give the longest repayment period but they provided some of the infrastructure I needed to implement other ideas. Think carefully about all aspects before you start changing things in your business.

- For every scrap of electricity we use there is a 5% VAT charge. Plus, all the money we use to pay for our fuel, gas, and electricity comes from money that is taxed. We work, and the government takes its share of tax – that is as it should be. However, if we can reduce our general running costs then we'll have greater disposable income. To put it in another way, if we bought a tax free investment that guaranteed a yield of 13.27% each year, we'd be jumping for joy!

I think many people are put off by the capital outlay of green technology, but I believe we can be smarter in our approach. I hope you can see how the approach of "Fire, Aim, Ready!" doesn't work, and how stopping to analyse can pay big dividends. I love green energy technology, but don't get caught up in the flashy gadgets – I listen to what the hard data is telling me. This same approach applies to any project, not just saving the planet.

If you are interested in learning how to make your house more energy efficient, I have a free e-learning course on my education website www.askjt.co.uk.

14

The Business of Students
Lean startup and business model canvas

How do you get 180 students to form into groups, come up with business ideas, and start trading in less than nine months?

Their objective would be to make money and to learn about what it's like to run a business for real.

For over eight years, I helped Northumbria University deliver a module called Graduate Enterprise. It was an exciting module that helped students set up a real business and run it for the academic year. In all, the module helped 1,584 students over ten years. During my time teaching, we had an average of 180 students each year. These students came onto the module cross-faculty, which means from different degree programs. We had students from business, fashion, design, computer science, sports, marketing, engineering, etc. We had 29 various degree programs feeding into the module at one point.

In short, that's over 30 businesses created each academic year to trade for nine months.

It was a little bit like herding cats.

By the way, as an undergraduate at a different university, I did the same module in 2003 and ended up starting my own business. My experiences gave me the necessary perspectives when I later went on to actually teach the module. I could relate to what the students were going through, and I was proof that it could work.

Be a rule breaker

The teaching team consisted of six people from different departments, and I was privileged to be one of them. I was the "entrepreneur" and I brought a connection between the real business world and academia, although many of the teaching staff also had excellent industry experience.

A common challenge within universities is that entrepreneurship doesn't always gel with the ethos of academic institutions. So I must commend Northumbria University for its bravery in running such a module. It was indeed a unique opportunity for students, and it showed the vocational and entrepreneurial focus of the university. The institution understood the importance of enterprise skills in employability, and the module provided a stepping stone for those wishing to start a business.

Still, the challenge remained. The university was keen to show its enterprise credentials, but that desire didn't always marry with other rules and regulations. You see, universities have complex franchise agreements with corporations like Starbucks. Universities love rules and regulations, such as the rule for no trading on campus. So what could go wrong with 180 students running around trying to set up businesses?! Especially when one of my student groups was selling coffee! Of course, I wasn't worried the group might topple the Starbucks empire, but the university would more than likely be concerned about their commercial agreements or health & safety considerations.

So to battle this problem, the university brought in Roger (I loved working with Roger). He managed the business support for students looking to start their own businesses after university. He told the students, in his hilarious way, everything they couldn't do. Such as no food, no alcohol, no sex, no electricity, no sex involving electricity, no crop spraying, etc. Now, I did deal with many exceptions to rules over the years, but I don't remember many people asking to do crop spraying. But plenty wanting to do electrical stuff (but without the sex).

We were backed by Young Enterprise, a national charity that helps young people gain essential enterprise skills. They provided some of the framework and most importantly, the insurance cover. We needed to keep the insurance people happy, and there were certain excluded trades. Overall, we had to make sure we didn't bring the university into disrepute and make certain the students were fully insured.

When delivering the module, one of our main jobs was informing students about all the things they weren't allowed to do. We wanted them to work within a set of rules and regulations so they'd become familiar with how the real business world worked. It would help them avoid problems in their future endeavours and keep them insurable.

I love rules because there is something satisfying about breaking a rule or two. As an entrepreneur, I look for wiggle room in rules. Despite the no food rule, we had many food businesses, including the coffee business. We simply had to consider how to *interpret* the rules. For example, one of the student groups told me that it had an excellent idea for a 3D-printed product. The university had 3D printers, and the students had a budget to spend across the year for academic projects.

My eyes lit up! "You're telling me you have a free manufacturing resource!"

However, the university rules said the equipment couldn't be used for commercial purposes. The student group asked me what they should do. Of course, to me, it was simple: they were part of a university module, so they were perfectly entitled to use the machines. Surely if they produced a couple of hundred prototypes, this would be fine, right? But seriously, at the time, 3D printers were costly, so there was no way I wanted my students to spend significant money and potentially end up with a loss. Yet the university may have denied using the machines if they had asked permission, or the permission process may have taken weeks. In the end, I provided the worldly wisdom of "It's easier to ask for forgiveness than gain permission" and "Just blame your module tutor if there is a problem" and off they went. The result of my approach led the students to win a regional competition and go on to a national one. Everyone was happy, and the university enjoyed the PR that was generated (and rightly so). Maybe they never realised I had tiptoed around the rules.

What this example and many others taught me was the realisation that the module was changing the students' outlook. I even remember a student coming up to me while I was eating lunch in the university canteen and declaring that one of the lectures I'd given had changed his entire outlook on his career. Wow! Our work was ground-breaking stuff.

My colleagues and I wanted as many groups as possible to be successful, specifically in terms of making a profit. As our journey to do this continued, I started to wonder about lean methodologies and how we could incorporate marginal gains.

Lean methodology is about looking at available, existing resources and maximising their use. Most importantly, it's about measuring and ensuring continuous improvement. A favourite book of mine, Eric Reis's *The Lean Startup*, looks at producing a "minimum viable product". This type of approach attracts early adopters to your business. A minimum viable product describes a product that has the bare minimum of features to gain traction in the marketplace. A student approached me a few years ago with the idea for a software tool. They told me they didn't have the money to pay for development and needed investment. I suggested they build a website to advertise the product and then push some marketing towards the website. When people clicked a sign up button they would be taken to a page where they'd enter an email address. They would then be informed when the product was ready. It's far easier to sell an investor on an idea if you have customers already waiting or if your website analytics show that people are interested in what you are doing. This marketing plan might seem extreme but when I had my web development business we used a brochure to advertise software products even though all of our products weren't yet developed or even in existence yet. Our job was to create or develop something only when we took on a client who desired that particular product or service. This was in 2004 – it's possible we might not get away with this approach now.

Eric Reis's book takes a scientific approach to startup, wherein you learn as you go and you're not afraid to make a few mistakes. Most importantly though, *The Lean Startup* is about measuring success against an objective you set. The ultimate goal is then to turn a minimal viable product into a feature-rich and fully finished product.

Lean methods are an exercise in innovation. But what does that mean when trying to get student businesses up and running?

How did we manage to get them all trading?

We had to get 180 students into groups of five or six, and they would then decide on their business idea. Looking back, the concepts of marginal gains and lean startup can be seen in our approach to creating teams, though we weren't initially aware of it. We experimented with the team formation process over the years, yet we'd not recognised that we were, in actuality, making marginal changes. We were always adapting our approach a little bit every year in order to make it more effective.

In the early years, we allowed groups to form from the same degree program. These were groups where everyone was already friends and from the same course, but this caused the issue that their range of skills were limited. For example, while business students might be stronger at business planning and finance, they lack technical skills such as web development, graphic design, and marketing implementation.

In another year, we'd tried a process whereby the teaching team decided on the groups. But our year over year measurements showed this didn't work as well. So we changed to a process whereby the students could form into groups with no more than three from the same faculty. At this point we realised we'd hit on the magic formula.

As far as teaching went, we had a business education curriculum delivered each week as lectures and a formula we would apply to get the students from A to B. My colleague Steve implemented techniques such as Belbin testing to help the students understand each other and the skills they had to offer. I developed a lecture about Myers-Briggs. The entire team worked together to create excellent material for sharing insights into marketing, teaching presentation skills, bringing in industry leaders to give talks, and educating about finance. Throughout everything, we always followed the thread of science and academic knowledge. The key point is that all of this consisted of minor adjustments. We were constantly measuring, testing, and implementing new ideas in order to increase the chance of success.

But we still had a big problem: we needed the students to be able to trade before Christmas. Christmas is a crucial period to make those all-important first sales, and it would be make or break for the success of the students' businesses. Furthermore, this was an academic module and we needed to award a mark to go towards a degree, so it had to contain academic rigour. We needed an assignment for them to do. So we required the student groups to prepare a business plan and a formal presentation. Business plans are complicated documents to prepare, and it was a lot to ask of the students. The students would have to submit the business plan and then deliver the presentation about their business right before Christmas. What's more, we were expecting them to not only prepare the plan but also trade and sell some of their products. They needed to source products, finance the purchase, and work out the pricing. They needed to design branding, build websites, and create a marketing plan. As you can imagine, it was a huge undertaking for the students to accomplish.

So, after a couple of years, I pitched an idea to my colleagues at the University that we should drop business plan documents. Madness! But see, I'd been reading about lean startup and lean methodologies. Instead of business plan documents, I suggested using something called a Business Model Canvas. A business model canvas is an A3 sheet of paper laid out as a business plan. The idea is that you can plan your business on one sheet of paper. To supplement this, we would ask the students to prepare additional pages on finances and basic market research. The objective was to get the students to work with the idea of a minimum viable product. A traditional business plan is about planning something to the nth degree. But with a business model canvas, we could speed up the process and move the students to the place of "Build, Measure, and Learn."

We took the onus away from time consuming business planning and instead gave the students a tool to help develop a business much quicker, so that they could get trading before Christmas. The intention was to take the focus off creating these large documents and put the emphasis on simply getting up and running. We dropped the presentations as well. Past students had been preparing PowerPoints and then presenting them to us through a formal assessment process. Instead, we organised a trade fair, during which the students had to give us an elevator pitch. Each student group had a trade stand, and we set a date before Christmas.

Many of these changes were examples of marginal gains. We were, in effect, introducing goal setting and enforced business deadlines rather than academic deadlines. Plus, the assessment process would result in them making some sales and recouping their capital investment. Part of the assessment process needed them to have an available product. This requirement exerted some necessary learning-environment pressure, but if they understood and utilised the concept of "lean," they had a realistic chance of being ready.

Don't forget that lean methodologies are about using the resources you already have. Lean Startup is not about doing things cheaply but about getting there quickly. So, did our new ideas and changes work? Yes! In the past we could only get half of the students trading before Christmas. But now we manage to get practically all of them doing so. Using marginal gains and implementing lean methodology, our teaching team improved at delivering the module.

The module produced students streets ahead of their peers. You could see from the jobs they gained after university that they could relate to real business issues. We'd given them what we call enterprise skills. As a potential employer, if you hear someone talk about real business issues in an interview, you understand that they have a deeper understanding of business. It was hardly surprising these students were getting better jobs. The module also helped some students clarify their interests and redirect their energies. Some students came into the module with well intentioned aspirations to set up their own businesses, but they realised after completing the module that it wasn't going to be for them.

Unfortunately, the module stopped being used because student surveys yielded results that were not particularly positive. Why might you ask? Some feedback we received showed that the students found running a business was difficult, full of uncertainty, and financially risky. Who knew??!! I found this quite entertaining, though it was sad that the module would end. Perhaps some of that feedback came from one particular worried student who asked me, "What happens if we lose money?"

"That's business," I replied.

The reality of losing money was real. It was why we'd experimented and tried different methods of doing things. But the module ultimately succumbed to the academic rigour I mentioned earlier. The concern that students showed in their feedback had more clout than the usefulness of those same students learning and experiencing real world truths about how difficult and uncertain it is to run a business.

It's noteworthy to add that before I was involved in the module, it was trialled only with computer science students who merely planned their business but never ran it. When surveyed at the end of that module, a high number of students indicated they would go on to start businesses – a far more significant proportion compared to students who did my team's module in subsequent years. This might sound like I'm diminishing the effectiveness of the changes my team brought, but from a learning perspective it showed something great. It showed that the *theoretical* reality of running a business often makes it seem safe, but once you experience it *for real* it can seem less appealing. And why would we want students starting real-world businesses to think it would be easy? The module that I was involved in during those subsequent years provided a safe yet realistic environment for students to trade in. And sometimes they learned that business wasn't for them. Two of my teaching team colleagues, Steve Ball and Dr Stephanie Macht, wrote a journal article in 2016. It's worth a read. They talk about how our module was authentic and student-centred. Their findings show that it's difficult to find academic material which looks at the practical reality of teaching enterprise skills. Maybe what we did was groundbreaking?

I've heard that the module has returned to the university, albeit in a slightly different form. It gladdens my heart to know authentic business education is still happening at the university, even though I'm no longer part of the teaching team.

I've talked about many subjects in this book. Yet, in some respects, the whole book is a conversation about lean methodologies and innovation. I think that learning about business in an academic environment makes it seem safe, but when you experience the actual running of one, even in a controlled environment, the risks become very real. The encouragement to experiment and measure is how we approached working with students, and this same approach can be transferred to the real world.

15

The Importance of Work
The science of people management

"**C**an I use the phone for a personal call," an employee asked.

"Yes, sure."

"Hi, I'm ringing about the AK-47. Is it still available?... It is. Great, let me call you back in 5 minutes."

He then turned to me and asked, "Is it ok if I get a parcel delivered to the office next week?"

It was 2005 and I'd only just employed my first member of staff. That was the moment I realised I was in deep trouble. This staff management business was going to be much more challenging than I first thought!

It was an airsoft gun but the mind, for a moment, boggles.

I've seen it all. Staff stealing money, body odour issues, inappropriate images on the company mobile phone, the list goes on. However, after some trial and mostly error, I had the makings of a great team. Loyal, dedicated, and passionate, with a great team spirit. I wasn't sure how I'd created this great team. Unfortunately, when my web development business closed in 2013, that team disbanded.

When I pressed the reset button and began my accountancy journey, I started to build a team again. A friend recommended a book called *Gung Ho* by Ken Blanchard, and I consumed it in a matter of hours. I realised that I had already done many of the things set out in the book back in my web business days. And these days, as I've returned to my scientific roots, I realise many of the concepts in *Gung Ho* (and other books I've read) are simply about psychology. To understand this area of science better would help me to create a fantastic team.

So what things was I good at back in my web business days? I was good at celebrating achievements, saying thank you, making an effort for people's birthdays, and being approachable. Small things perhaps. Yet, for example, the act of saying thank you has been studied and has been shown to have a profound effect on the person saying the words, the recipient, and anyone else who witnesses it. While Ken's book doesn't really spell out the science, I believe this example reflects that even simple acts have an effect that goes back to psychology.

Since then I have pledged to become even better at saying thank you – I make sure I go out of my way to say things like "Well done," "Thank you," and "Brilliant job." When someone takes on a job outside their comfort zone, I take time to say how proud I am of their development. As the head of a company, I make sure to thank the whole team if we have a great month. Even buying some food for the team and taking time out to celebrate has become more significant for me. That said, giving thanks to someone must be genuine. You can't fake it. Ok, maybe you can initially, since humans aren't great at picking up false information. But I believe that if you are faking it, it will bite you on the backside in the long run.

What about the stuff I hadn't been good at?

While I did have a great team in my web development business, it wasn't problem-free. I still had issues with staff members wanting to assume responsibility and resolve their own problems.

The first stage I tackled with my new team was to help the staff realise why work is worthwhile and important. I spend time with all new members of staff explaining why the work we do is critical and why they should feel it is important.

As humans, our brains are wired to find meaning in our lives. A raft of psychology research shows that there is a connection between mental illness and the inability to find such meaningfulness or having a lack of belief in a value system.

Here is a little story about what my work means to me, to help you understand why our work, whatever it is, needs to be worthwhile and important:

Into my office comes a massive chap, tattoos up the arms, bearded, big muscles, and a deep voice. This railway worker says he'd made a huge mistake and HMRC were chasing him for £3,000 of penalties!

"I've got some letters from HMRC in the car, but I'm too frightened to open them," he explained.

Too frightened! This man surely isn't frightened of anything and must eat nine Weetabix for breakfast. So I made him go down to the car to get the letters and I opened them for him. To cut a long story short, it turned out he'd been unwell and I helped him write a penalty appeal, which he won.

What an amazing day! The client became one of our brand champions and has referred many clients to us. I could have submitted a standard penalty appeal letter but I didn't. I analysed the situation and spent time doing worthwhile work. The critical takeaway for me was that people worry about things like taxes but I am able to take that pain and stress away from them.

That letter was the best work I could do. I don't enjoy writing penalty appeal letters but I know they are critical. In the North East of England, £3,000 of penalties is a significant sum of money for many people. For this client, the penalty represented 14% of the client's annual income.

The stakes couldn't be higher, so while I don't like such letters, I put all my efforts into the client's work. This effort, this choice to do my best, provides me the opportunity to do work that feels truly meaningful.

"I feel like a weight has been lifted just talking to you," he told me after the end of the first meeting, when I'd opened the letters.

It's interesting how an initial meeting can create a sense of relief for the client. I was able to take away a problem. And even though I explained to the client that he might not be successful, it didn't matter because, in his eyes, someone was simply trying to help him.

By the way, my view of HMRC is often different to how others view them. In my experience, the inspectors we deal with are professionals just like me. They are reasonable, they work to a high standard, and they're usually very pleasant. The story above is a good case in point – the client had a valid reason to appeal and won because an HMRC professional applied some common sense. However, clients usually hold a totally opposite view of HMRC and are often terrified of them. I believe it's our job to help clients manage that kind of emotion and worry. So if I can build a business where our staff is understanding, knowledgeable, and caring, we'll have the capacity to transform a client's life by eliminating or reducing fear and stress. Who wouldn't want to work for someone doing this kind of magical work?

Don't think for a moment that the idea that work is worthwhile and important doesn't apply to the work that *you* do, whatever it may be. Imagine you're a cleaner. Often viewed as the bottom rung in an organisation. Yet when clients walk into an office they will draw opinions of cleanliness and tidiness. A clean office keeps my team healthy and motivated. A cleaner's work is worthwhile and important, but have you ever told them so? Why not take a moment to say thank you and explain why what they do is critical. Does your team realise what the cleaner does is essential to the business?

Celebrating people and understanding why work is important are fairly easy notions to implement, but the next stage is the hard bit.

Being Challenged and Team Spirit

The next stage of the team development plan was to make my team autonomous. To make them a team that could react, think for themselves, and understand the organisation's boundaries. To create a team spirit that would be hard to beat. My team is the gateway to me having the work-life balance my children and wife deserve. It's this creation of team spirit that is the hard bit, and achieving it requires some intangibles.

For my business, I wrote a set of values (perhaps you could call them beliefs) that set the bar high. Yet I also wanted them to be values that everyone could buy into. Team members need to buy into values and beliefs, and they should be some of the first things they learn and experience when starting their jobs. And that begins at the top – if you have a set of values for the organisation, as a leader you must live by them yourself.

My Values and Beliefs

I challenge staff rather than giving straight answers to questions. I coach and mentor. I teach by using advanced questioning techniques. Whoever said answering a question with a question is bad manners was wrong! It's a powerful teaching technique that is underutilised. I ask people to suggest solutions to problems and to share the reasons why they think they might work. I encourage other members of staff to coach each other, especially when we have a new apprentice.

I openly discuss profitability and the challenges the business faces. Staff have access to our profit and loss. Most of these people are accountants, so they can comprehend that type of information. It's not just profitability the staff see, but also information relating to performance. Stuff like how many proposals we send, what percentage of those proposals we win, how much time is spent on each client, etc. All that data analysis I discussed in an earlier chapter – they see that information, too.

Of course, each business is different. You'll need to consider how information will be presented in your particular organisation. For me, I have a well-educated team capable of understanding complex information. Therefore, I believe I can share aspects of the bigger picture, and because my team can see that, they can make decisions without my input.

One day my colleague Adam said to me, "Justin, we're not getting proposals sent to new clients quick enough. I've looked at how long it takes us and how it needs improvement." I'm the boss, yet here was a relatively new member of staff suggesting how to improve our business. It was only because he had access to information that he could reach his conclusion.

I always ask my team members for input into decisions, and I always ask for opinions during our team meetings. Everything is up for debate and can be challenged. I listen, and I try to act on what people say to me. Imagine turning your workplace into a constant dialogue about improvement and discussing openly what's not going well. Especially when decisions can be made based on facts and information that are readily accessible to all.

To support such autonomy, we offer training opportunities for development, usually via the UK government apprenticeship program. This program will amaze you with what's available (all the way up to full degrees).

This is a big part of people working *with* you rather than *for* you. There's a huge difference. If people only work for you they need constant direction; they look to you for every decision. When people are working with you they become autonomous, all working with shared goals in mind.

Magic starts to happen when you get this right. For example, one of my business values is to tell clients about any mistakes we make, especially as I believe it's rare that a mistake can't be undone or fixed.

My colleague Chris said to me, "I don't think I've given the right advice to a client."

Music to my ears, though some business owners would be horrified.

"Ok!" I replied, "Let's sit down and talk it over. What happened?"

Chris understood our values and expectations, and he felt he could bring a stressful concern about a mistake to me. We resolved things, because it turned out he hadn't given duff advice but merely needed to explain it a little better.

Our business's environment of openness and dialogue led to a great opportunity for me to coach and mentor Chris. Similarly, I've noticed my team looking at the management accounts and asking questions about how we can reduce costs. I've seen staff members chasing debt and pushing for direct debit signups. The magic is that I never really asked them to do it. They understood it was mission critical to the business and they understood how I wanted the business to run, so they took their own initiative.

As we've become a bigger organisation I can't do everything, and I find my knowledge in certain areas isn't as good as it used to be. I ask members of my team to check my own work and to challenge what I've done. It would be stupid of me to think I was perfect at everything.

This in itself shows that the boss is part of the team and sees value in what other team members have to offer.

Before you rush off to implement everything, there are a few more ideas to share. You have to live and breathe all these ideas. Not just for a week or two, but all the time. There are no half measures and no cutting corners when something doesn't suit you. Creating team spirit has been years of hard work.

I'm going to use the next few chapters to look at some of the other ideas I've implemented. Ideas like having a value system and the power of processes. You now have some tools from Chapter 14 about my journey with students. You now understand personality types and how understanding the brain can give you a better insight into people. This insight makes you better at handling people, because it's about psychology, and psychology is science, and science works!

The problem with commissions

Creating a team is amazing, but what about paying those team members? What about incentives (remember those)? I can't move on without discussing how we pay people. Money can be a motivator, and motivation sits firmly within the realm of science.

I'm the Financial Director of a letting agency, and one day my co-director rang me in a flat panic. We had two lettings negotiators (these are sales people who let properties) who were on a low basic salary but a good commission structure. Let's call them Tim and Jenny. Tim, one of the negotiators, had let a property and arranged for the tenants to come in later in the afternoon to sign the paperwork and pay the deposit. He was super excited as this was the let that would move his commission to the next tier.

The issue was that Jenny had a different tenant interested in taking the same property. She picked up the phone and told them they needed to get down to the office straight away to pay the deposit. Jenny told the tenant that her colleague had someone coming in the afternoon to sign the paperwork, cutting them out of securing the property. Needless to say, Jenny's tenants rushed down to the office and signed up. Jenny didn't say anything to Tim.

Later that afternoon the other tenants arrived to see Tim and sign up for their dream home. Jenny popped her head round the corner and very calmly said, "Oh I let that property this morning, didn't you know?" World War III erupted in the office.

Why did it happen? I asked her why she'd just cut the other negotiator out of the deal in this manner. She explained, "You pay our commission separately so I thought we were in competition with each other." Her actions resulted in a complaint from the tenants who lost out on the property. The complaint took weeks to sort out, and she'd ruined her relationship with her colleague. It was appalling.

It was this situation that led me to look at the science of incentives to answer the question "Do they really work?" The situation showed that the incentive had produced an effect but also resulted in a negative outcome. I despaired that two so-called teammates would almost throw each other under the bus to gain more commission. If we paid them a larger salary would they perform better?

I suggested to the team the idea of implementing a larger salary without a commission structure. I was confronted with an expected answer: "But commissions are how the industry works!" However, the key problem earlier had been that Tim and Jenny were working towards their own goals and serving their own values. Rather than the goals and values of the business. They were clearly working *for* us and not *with* us.

When you set differing targets and incentives for each member of staff, you put them in competition with each other. This approach doesn't feed into the overall business objectives. The members of staff become fixated on achieving their personal incentives, sometimes with unethical behaviour, as we saw with Jenny.

So I came up with a solution.

Profit Shares

In the last few years I implemented one final step for my organisation. I've talked about incentives and how I don't think they really work. However, before I was familiar with the science regarding incentives, my accountancy business implemented a killer scheme to motivate the troops. At the same time as I was building that team, I started making good money. I had a good work life balance; things were great. So I thought, "What about the people who work for me?" They were paid fairly but that was it. Now you might think this part of my story is a little egalitarian or socialist but...

I decided to share 50% of the profit with the staff.

This is the rough premise of how it works. My wife Sue and I are fee earners for the business so I decided we would be included in the 50% split. It did initially mean that we got more than 50% of the profit. However, as the team has expanded, our shared proportion as business owners has decreased. This is the egalitarian bit: I took the approach of an equal split for all staff – in effect, everyone receives the same amount. This has the effect of boosting the lower paid and junior members of staff in terms of their salary. As a junior member of staff your salary is lower so a profit share would be advantageous. That's my thinking anyway.

So why did I go down this route?

I came across some research published in 2008 by the National Bureau of Economic Research which told me that profit sharing would generate some positive results. The study looked at 40,000 employees across 14 different companies, so it was a great sample size and a good source. The more research I found on profit sharing the more encouraged I became. I was looking to add to my mantra of getting the staff to understand the expectations and to think for themselves. And to build that all important team spirit.

I'd always admired the John Lewis model of business wherein the employees are partners. I knew incentives and commissions were likely to fail so I was interested to find out more about profit sharing models. I already had many things right in my team. They understood why work was important, they understood the values of the business, and they saw the important difference between profit and caring. They had access to key financial information and other management information. Surely, adding a profit share would further enhance this level of autonomy.

Then I came across something else that made me realise it all could *really* work.

Dean Price of Gravity Payment in the U.S decided to increase all his employees' base salaries to $70,000 in April 2015. This could be viewed as a social experiment. However, he was not a socialist but rather a man of science. He came across some interesting research from 2010 by Daniel Kahneman and Angus Deaton. It indicated that emotional well-being levelled off at a $70,000 salary level, but at rates up to $70,000 emotional well-being could increase dramatically.

The research supports the idea that an increase in salary corresponds to an increase in social well-being. Therefore, it makes sense to share profit equally so those on the lowest salary have the greatest rise in emotional well-being.

A 2021 research paper by Matthew Killingsworth similarly indicates that amounts over $75,000 can create rises in emotional well-being, though he warns not to over-interpret the data. I personally think it supports the evidence of Kahneman & Deaton and confirms the science.

Does a profit share work? I think so. It's always tough to say without undertaking some form of detailed study, but in my business I see a loyal team working to a common goal of success. I observe a team interacting with management information to draw conclusions and make their own decisions. They understand the importance for analysis and efficiency. I do believe you first have to get many of the other aspects right before profit sharing becomes a strategy. You need to implement things like values, ethics, good mentoring, and a good company ethos before profit shares should be considered. Even my own profit share scheme has gone through various iterations over the last 2 years. That said, I've now settled on a model which I think works best.

Before I move on, I want to say something about referral fees. Why mention referral fees at this stage? It's all part of the profit sharing ethos and values we have as an organisation. I think it sets a good example to the team that while profit is brilliant there are limits we have to set.

I'm offered referral fees all the time when I introduce clients to people like solicitors, mortgage advisors, and independent financial advisors. Our business could be remunerated very handsomely through negotiating business deals. (Last year we made referrals that would have been worth over £1M). However, I never felt the ethics were right to do so. The client is already paying a fair fee – should we be taking cash under the table? Would our clients be happy if we disclosed it? Finally, how can I stay an impartial advisor if I'm being paid? Would taking referral fees stay true to our values?

We stick to our values. It might be right for another business but it doesn't work for us.

I often encourage the team to do something for a client even though it doesn't generate a profit. If the client is struggling, maybe offering that helping hand is the right thing to do rather than charging a fee. It is a careful balancing act which doesn't always work. As long as we can acknowledge the things that haven't worked then we can improve for the future.

Could you do it in your own business?

Highly complex structures are needed to operate profit shares. But like me, you can keep Occam's razor in mind and always look for the simple. For example, I run it all through the payroll, not through some elaborate share scheme.

It's also necessary to pay people a fair basic salary before instituting a profit share. It means you need accurate management accounts, and you'll need to be able to produce those documents before you can even consider a profit share. I work three months in arrears to give time for adjustments to profit.

Another consideration is the calculating of the profit and how it gets divided up. For example, if a member of staff only works part time, then they get a proportion of profit relative to the hours worked by a full time member of staff.

It's not easy for me to manage the profit share for the staff. It's not in the employment contract but done at my discretion. This gives me control if something unexpected happens, yet on the whole I'm probably more generous than I need to be. Honestly, I only have my success because of these wonderful people! Even the proceeds of this book fall into the profit share so my staff will take part in any success it has. Let's hope that happens!

A word of warning!

Don't read this chapter and think that I get everything right. I don't, and I doubt I ever will. I'll be forever adjusting and trying to improve. We're playing with psychological and cognitive science that is highly complex. (See: the thousands of journal articles written on the subject.)

I just want to say this: when I ask my clients what they think of our team, the answer is "Fantastic!"

I could write an entire book just about staff management and this chapter only scratches the surface, but hopefully you can draw some ideas from it and consider the questions I've raised.

16

Do you drink milk?
The power of values & leadership

In the previous chapter, I discussed how I have tried to create a killer team in my accountancy business. I talked about implementing profit sharing and celebrating successes for the purpose of developing team spirit. Yet from early on in my team building efforts I felt like something more was necessary. I came to realise that I would need some kind of special sauce to bring everyone together.

If someone had told me in my mid-20s that having a belief system within an organisation was critical to its success, I'd have laughed. But I've realised that beliefs are very important – because all business owners bring certain ones with them into their ventures. These beliefs turn into values, and these values usually make their way into the fabric of a business.

If you read the numerous psychology articles about getting teams to function, one word keeps appearing: values. A lot of research points to the importance of values in creating a corporate culture. That might sound like a load of corporate nonsense, but let me prove it to you with a story about milk.

Do you drink milk?

"I don't trust anyone, so why should I trust you?" a potential client challenged me.

"How's the cup of tea?" I answered.

"Excuse me?"

"Well, one of my team members made that cup of tea for you. So you must have some trust in people. Even more, it has milk in it."

"What the hell has milk got to do with it?!" He was getting annoyed.

"Do you know how many people are involved in getting that milk bottle to our office? Milk is a business of trust, and hundreds of people are involved in the supply chain. Any one of them could have interfered with it."

My point is that the client and I had different values. I trust people, but it didn't seem like he did. The client wouldn't have fit with our organisation's values; we'd have been fighting with each other from the very start. I didn't win the work, but I'm not sure I wanted it. Why would I work for someone who believed the world was against them? Some people will decree that any client is a good client, but I've been down that path before, thinking I could work for anyone. I'll let one of my competitors learn that particular lesson with this client!

I value trust. I choose to trust people (even after a member of staff stole from me). I continue to trust that the vast majority of society is made up of decent human beings. But how does this translate into a workplace?

What do you hate?

I want you to consider everything you hate about a terrible customer service experience. I deliberately use the word "terrible" because when we have terrible experiences, they are usually representative of moments where two differing value systems are in very strong contrast with each other.

Personally, I value effort and commitment, so I hate it when someone just doesn't care.

This was brought into focus when I decided to order a new campervan. We went to a local dealer who had been advertising a fantastic event featuring an international manufacturer. So we turned up on a Saturday morning first thing. What did we encounter? Well, the staff weren't interested in us being there. No one said good morning, everyone was moping around, and they looked miserable. We had a van in mind so we took a good look at it, spending 20 minutes checking if it would be suitable for us. Yet not a single member of staff came over to ask if we needed help or had questions.

Undaunted, I told my wife, "Let's go speak to the sales manager."

So off we went, excited, into the sales office, ready to buy something extraordinary. (It certainly came with an extraordinary price tag!)

"I sold all of those yesterday! The event started on Friday didn't you know?" said the sales manager.

He was not pleased to see us and continued to work on his computer. In the hope that we would leave.

"Oh! But what about more stock in the future, as the van is perfect for our needs? Is there a waiting list?" I asked.

"No!" came the answer as he bashed away on the keyboard. "Don't know, maybe you should try a different dealer," he added.

When looking at paying £50,000 for a new campervan, I was hoping for some excellent service, or at least something decent. I also had an existing van to sell, which would have been a perfect opportunity for them to be helpful and to make money. Plus, I had servicing requirements. So many opportunities for them. You would hope the team would have been a little more enthusiastic to see us. You can buy a house in the North East of England for less than that amount!

It wasn't my first interaction with this dealer. I'd tried to get them to service my existing van, but that was more or less impossible. On another occasion, when we were looking to buy our first van, they had double booked our appointment and we were asked to leave. No mention of "Is there another van we can show you?" or "What are you looking for?" or "Can we arrange another time?"

I can't be sure, but I assume issues regarding leadership and values were at the heart of their deficiencies. In a small business, everything comes from the top – the actions and values at the top inevitably get transferred to the entire team.

So what can you do?

I've always wanted a fantastic team with the most incredible drive for customer service. And to help with that, I strive to give them knowledge and responsibility in return.

So I established these beliefs:

- **We coach and mentor our staff and our clients.** This is our most important belief.
- We work with people with the goal of enabling and empowering them.
- We believe people are, on the whole, good and honest. Just remember milk!
- We believe authority is earned through behaviour, not just by the fact that someone has a particular job title.
- If we truly get to know someone, we can help them overcome their challenges in order to enhance their strengths.

- ❀ We believe a better future can only be achieved by working together.
- ❀ *No*, *can't*, and *impossible* are words that are not included in our long term business outlook.
- ❀ People who have worked for the business should look back on their time with us as positive and meaningful.

There's a difference between values and beliefs. On the one hand, values are what we deem to be important, things like diversity, honesty, integrity, education, loyalty, etc. You can understand values as the overall standards to which you work. On the other hand, a belief is just something you think to be true, even if there isn't any proof to support it. For me, my values ultimately stem from my belief system. For this reason I've always chosen to share my belief system with my team.

I've always had people prepared to follow me and show great loyalty. Once you establish values and a great ethos towards team management, you'll have a killer formula for success.

The challenge with values is that you need to live by them.

We believe we should be a helpful organisation. It's easy to say "that's not part of our service" or "we can't do that because it's not our area of expertise," but I've always tried to impress upon my team that if we can help, we should. For example, when a client asks me about legal problems, the easy way out is to say we're an accountancy business, not a firm of solicitors. However, I always try to offer some words of wisdom, then usually follow up by giving an introduction to a solicitor I trust.

Instilling these sorts of values and methods for working throughout a business starts at the top. It all comes down to leadership.

Leadership

I consider myself to be a good leader, and the people around me tell me as much. I've never had a problem getting people to follow me, and I've never really given it much thought.

There is a big difference between leadership and management. I've sometimes been sceptical about whether leadership can be taught. I've tended to believe it's only possible to teach management skills.

So, where did my ability to lead come from? Was I just born a leader?

In my early teenage years, I was a boy with no confidence. That boy is still there today, but few ever get to see him and his cracks of doubt.

To explain how we go from the boy with no confidence to a confident leader, I need to tell you a story. I've been on one long leadership training program over the last 27 years, except I didn't have to pay for it and I didn't even realise I was on it!

My leadership training started when I joined the Army cadet force at age 13. I followed a program set out by the army – taking tests on weapons handling, being given responsibility, and being rewarded with cadet ranks as I progressed. By age 17, I'd worked my way up to the rank of Colour Sergeant. In my final year, I was asked to become Head of Section. This meant that I was ordered to take control of my unit.

From the age of 13 to 18, the army pushed me into team tasks, and everyone at some point had the opportunity to take on the role of squad leader. I did classroom work to become an NCO (non commissioned officer) which gave me the knowledge to train junior cadets. That training then gave me the responsibility to teach weapons handling.

After becoming Head of Section, I was suddenly required to get my peers to follow me. If I gave an order, they had to follow it. All these small opportunities were training me to become a leader.

But guess what? At 17 years old, I sometimes couldn't get my peers to show me respect or fall in line when I told them to. I experimented with different techniques when they didn't do what I wanted. Don't forget that it was the army, so push-ups, shouting, and long runs were the go-to options for convincing people.

But I noticed that some cadets did as they were asked without needing much encouragement. I didn't think about it then, but I had gained their respect. I had worked hard to be given the responsibility to teach weapons handling and to achieve ranks that others were still working towards. I had the ear of the sergeant major and the respect of teachers, including those who held an officer's rank.

It's strange to think back to that time as I can now see the many mistakes I made. Yet I realise that the cadets who followed me were the ones I was consistently fair with. See, I don't think I was always fair with everyone. But at the age of 17, I still wasn't an adult and still had a lot to learn.

I've already said there's a massive difference between people working *for* you and people working *with* you. In the office, I see myself as part of the team. Rarely do I see myself as the boss. Sure, other people see me as the boss because I'm the head of the organisation. Someone has to be! But I'm interested in a different dynamic. You can be the head of an organisation by title yet not have the team's respect. If that's the case, you're not in control. The title of Director can be easily given but takes time to earn. It was the same when I was in the cadets. I needed to earn the respect of the other cadets just like I now need to earn the respect of my team.

When we consider leadership, we see the need for intelligence, drive, empathy, an ability to spot emotions in ourselves and others, curiosity, humility, and values.

When we track my leadership experience, it began with setting up a business at 21. I started employing people at the age of 23. I made huge mistakes and was making it up half the time. But all the leadership experience, including all the errors, has made me a much better leader today. I watched my mum lead her team in her own business, which itself was an experience. Throughout everything I was on a continuous leadership training program. I hope you can glean something from my stories and the journey I've been on.

Early in my business career, I learned a lot from one particular leader. I had the great privilege to go to events where I saw senior business leaders speak. One of these speakers was the CEO of a FTSE 100 company. Even though it was 17 years ago, he left me with an everlasting memory that I continue to draw on. It was his humility and humbleness. He wasn't arrogant and full of his own self-importance. When he was asked a question about his long-term future in the business, he simply replied that if someone better came along, he'd need to stand aside. Research indicates that humility is an essential trait of strong leaders. In his 2001 book *Good to Great*, Jim Collins found humility to be a common trait among CEOs who had taken businesses from average performance to superior advantage in the market.

Dr. Robert Hogan is a psychologist we should also listen to on this front. He is considered one of the greatest living psychologists. His research and writing on the subject of leaders make him the world's most influential psychologist on leadership. He highlights that humble leaders make the best leaders, even though they are often overlooked by those with more charismatic traits.

When you're searching for leaders that you can bring into your own business, you may need to look at using a recruiting method that leaves any of your personal biases at the door. Explore bringing humility into your own leadership style and observe what happens.

In the end, leadership can indeed be taught! I'm most likely proof of it. Research also agrees. In 2015 a meta-analysis published in the British Psychology Journal indicated that leadership skills improved when leadership training was undertaken. (A meta-analysis is an analysis of multiple journal articles that address the same question.)

To implement the ideas in this chapter, create a robust belief system and be a humble leader. If things go wrong, don't despair. See it as an experience that will make you a better leader. You can expect to feel doubt as you learn to lead, but that's all part of it. That feeling of doubt is to be expected as a leader, but over time you will come to accept it or at the very least understand it.

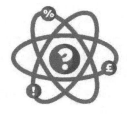

17

Wash your hands!
The power of process

How do you get the rate of infections to decrease in a hospital?

Simple: get the caregivers to wash their hands!

You know about Occam – simple ideas are the best – and you've learned about innovation. Now I want to show how process innovations can be the simplest and easiest to implement. They can be a bit boring, but once you see their impact, you'll realise the results are not dull.

Many years ago I came across a newspaper article about an American doctor who had reduced operating theatre mortality rates by a third. A third!

What had caused the dramatic drop in deaths?
A checklist!

Not a new invention, not a new drug, but a checklist. The doctor conducting the study didn't believe the results when they were analysed, so he made his research assistant recheck. Still the same. Furthermore, the same study was done in both developed and developing countries – with the exact same results. The results of using a checklist wasn't affected by the wealth of the country in which the study was done. Interesting! The doctor who conducted the study is named Atul Gawande. He published his work in a medical journal and wrote a book called *The Checklist Manifesto*. It's a fantastic book that can change your perspective on our complex lives.

Let's go back to my original question of infection control. Would you put hand washing high on the list? Of course you would, but unless it is written into a process, people won't always follow it. The studies prove it: you can prevent 24 - 40% of diarrhoea cases just with better hand hygiene.

But where is the process that ensures hand hygiene takes place at the most appropriate interval?

By the way, there have been experiments with hospital signage in order to improve the hand washing rates for visitors. They must have seen the study of hotel signage and towel washing!

I want you to get one thing clear in your mind now. It is impossible to get things right without a process. Don't fight me on that statement. It's true.

Firstly, if you want people to wash their hands, that's one thing, but getting them to do it *at the right moment* involves following a process.

Secondly, it's impossible to get things perfectly right in our modern businesses. The level of complexity we face is eye-watering. We've all read about lawyers, doctors, pilots, computer programmers, etc. making catastrophic mistakes. These people study and train for years, have years of on-the-job experience, and undertake professional development training to keep their skills up to date, yet they still make catastrophic mistakes.

Do you remember the Deepwater Horizon blowout in April 2010 that killed 11 people and brought about a huge underwater oil spill? This catastrophic disaster was fundamentally caused by a series of errors due to a lack of processes.

An interesting 2011 Harvard Business Review article examines how human brains are wired to misinterpret and ignore warnings. Ultimately, we have to accept that unless we implement structure and clearly outlined ways of working, mistakes will happen.

The trouble is, no one wants to allow mistakes. So how do we stop them from happening?

The simple way for most businesses is to utilise a checklist. It serves as a type of process.

In a small business, it can be tricky to find the time to write down what you're doing, i.e. which steps need to be carried out to perform a task and the details of how to do them. Therefore, writing a list is a simple way to quickly start the business towards being process-led. Simply make a list and add a ticky box to each item on it. I have a skilled team who already understands how to apply their skills to a job – we just needed a way to prompt them to apply the knowledge at the right moment. Checklists!

Most big businesses will already have these sorts of systems in place. However, they are often programmed into a highly complex software system. But don't worry, small businesses don't need fancy computer systems. There's nothing wrong with a simple piece of paper.

Why build a process?

This chapter is really about processes in general, not just checklists. That said, I'm going to focus slightly more on checklists because they are the simplest way to get you on the right track towards a better business.

Developing a process for your business is going to help with two things:

1. Improving the retention and sharing of knowledge
2. Improving accuracy (reducing catastrophic errors)

Improving the retention and sharing of knowledge

As my team has grown, I've found I can't always be around to answer questions. And while my team is fantastic and great at assisting new staff, it's particularly frustrating and inefficient to be interrupted all the time when they have questions.

Therefore, we developed a document called the New Starter Guide. It's full of helpful stuff and it's split into two sections. The first section is about the organisation – our values, customer service, focus on health & well being, and simple stuff like the names of each staff member and their contact details. The second section is about how to undertake specific basic tasks. For example: how to login to your email, what to do with confidential waste, data protection policies, and the ever-exciting explanation of how to call HMRC.

We spent a considerable amount of time developing this document. All the staff members who have used it agree it is helpful and prevents them from feeling lost during their early months of working with us.

In short, this *process* document has taken a snapshot of our knowledge and documented it for future use. It saves time because staff members don't need to do so much refresher training. It's easy to share and read and provides us with documented, well-established best practices.

All that said, I could be better! I admit it – I'm guilty as charged. I don't have enough written processes, but I've decided to focus on the 80/20 rule – the most important aspects of a process are captured where they matter most. In this case, a new starter document doesn't tell a new recruit everything about our business, but it gets them started on the right foot with the most essential knowledge.

Improving Accuracy

After reading the journal article on checklists by Atul Gawande I realised that I could apply the same principles in my business. We developed a series of checklists – we call them TRQs (Tax Return Questionnaires). They ask all the critical questions we need to know, and we revisit them often to change and update the questions.

For a long time we have been compiling a list of all the problems we encounter when completing tax returns for people. Problems such as missing dates of birth or national insurance numbers, not knowing the number of dependents or marriage status, or not being informed about charitable donations or loans. The list goes on. The task of tax reporting is very complex because every individual is entirely different in terms of their work, benefits package, pension arrangements, investment choices, etc. The number of permutations of a tax return is incalculable (and I imagine this is true in any country). So what we did was turn the entire tax return into a checklist.

I deduced most clients would have the same mix of income areas such as employment, self employment, and property. Therefore, we would include more items on the checklists in these areas. The less common tax areas or where specialist knowledge is needed were just single tick boxes. This meant that if we happened to tick one of the more complex or less familiar areas of tax, we could pick it up later and ensure we focused on it.

Let me give you an example: In the UK, once your earnings reach £50,000, you need to start repaying something called Child Benefit. Therefore, having questions on the checklist about how many children a client has and what the children's ages are makes sense. This reminds us to bring the legislation to the client's attention and ensure they don't get a nasty tax surprise.

We've since extended our checklists to include requirements for preparing end-of-year accounts. We sometimes take over accounts from other accountants and half of them don't even state correct bank balances! Guess what the first question on our checklist is: Is the bank reconciled at the year-end, and does it match the bank statement? This might seem simple, but you'd be amazed by the simple stuff that gets overlooked.

Our office has a rule: we don't do work for people until one of these checklists is completed. Why? We have learned from experience that if we make assumptions about a client and don't complete a checklist, something will go wrong. As we've grown as a business and taken on more clients, it has become impossible for us to keep every client's affairs in our heads. These checklists act as a way to quickly understand the client and to ensure we provide advice at the right time.

Our own checklist forms started out on paper and we completed them by pen during our initial client meeting.

Later, we turned the checklist forms into PDFs and uploaded them onto an iPad for use with an Apple pencil. We could then email them directly to the people who would deal with them next. We started with the simplicity of pen and paper and added complexity later. And keep in mind that the checklist is one part of the process, while the step of sending the form to the appropriate people is another.

The opportunity to mentor and advise

My most important belief is to coach and mentor our staff and clients. I discovered checklists were a tool for doing just that, and they allowed me to coach and advise at the right moments.

Let me use pension contributions as an example. In the case of a client who is a 40% taxpayer, a certain tax relief may be available if they put money into their pension. The person might not know about this potential tax relief, yet the awareness of it may prompt them to contribute to a pension. So if one of my clients fits this situation, my tax knowledge opens up the door for me to provide them with advisory services. Though our business doesn't offer financial advice about products like pensions, taking the opportunity to do a quick bit of extra, helpful education will be valuable for that client for years to come.

Another great example: we have three questions at the end of our TRQ checklist form that have nothing to do with the services our business provides. One of these questions asks if clients have a Last Will and Testament. No one likes the idea of dying, yet we sometimes have to face the fact that the worst can happen. I have seen some terrible cases of children being put into care following the death of a single parent because a Will hadn't been made! It's one of the most catastrophic mistakes that can be made, and it has terrible consequences. Therefore, to make my clients aware of such risks and to help them protect their loved ones, I built a question about Wills into my checklist. We wouldn't be the provider of the particular service, but the checklist question served to fulfil our stated goal of advising clients whenever we could.

What about other industries?

One of our clients, the director of a construction company, told me about the challenges they faced when undertaking work in people's houses. They often couldn't get various aspects of the job correct. So I invited them round to my house to give me a quote for a bathroom refit. They sent a member of their team who was knowledgeable and enthusiastic about bathrooms. He took down loads of measurements on a piece of paper and then went away to work on the quote. The quote came through and was split into two elements: materials and labour. I'll mention that I thought the estimate for the labour seemed too low.

I followed up a few days later with the director and asked some questions:

- Can you tell me what the floor is made of?
- Where is the stop tap to the house?
- Where is the main circuit box for the home?
- Is there an isolator for the water supply in the bathroom itself?

- What is the access like to the property? How far will the delivery drivers have to go, and are there any steps?
- How much rubbish removal would there be from the job, and where is the nearest location for a skip?
- Are there any existing leaks?
- What is the age of the house?
- Is the hot water a gas boiler or tank? Are there any utility issues?

The director asked me why all these things mattered.

I told him that there was an existing leak in the bathroom that might be compromising the floorboards. I also informed him that the job would require the delivery to go up a narrow staircase, and that there'd be a 150-metre carry for all the materials. Ditto for the rubbish removal.

Suddenly the penny dropped for the director. It became apparent to him that although the employee who had come to do the measurements was great, he wasn't the person who'd be doing the work. He started to imagine how beneficial it would be if answers to all the questions could be provided to the fitting team before it arrived on site. He realised they could create a standard checklist or form that would eliminate the problems they kept facing time after time. One such problem being labour costs (remember that estimate I mentioned?) often becoming much higher than initially quoted, something that customers didn't appreciate.

Where to start?

The best place to start with your processes is at the beginning of your customer's journey with you. It has become very fashionable to call this "onboarding."

What does my business's "onboarding" journey look like?

- We complete our checklist form with the client. This gathers all personal information (name, address, DOB, etc.) but also asks all the key questions to complete their tax work.
- This form is digital on an iPad and is immediately emailed to two other people. These two people are responsible for quoting and administration. It has allowed me to delegate the job of onboarding to others in my team.
- The number of sections we complete on this form allows us to apply a formula to the price. Therefore, although I've met the client, I don't have to personally send them the quote or be involved in this step.
- As soon as the client accepts the proposal, an automated notice informs the admin person who then saves the document to a shared folder. They can then begin getting the client set up on the system and undertaking tax registrations, since we've already collected the information upfront.

The above points are just a precis of what a written process should look like. The checklist form is just one step in that process.

The example reveals one of the real benefits we've had with our own checklists: being able to move toward formulaic pricing. How I complete the questionnaire determines the prices we quote for a job. This then removed me from the pricing. The checklist form contains all the stuff we need to onboard clients. We can then deploy a more in-depth process document to deal with the new client administration work, which allows it to be delegated to someone else.

In short, we have a slick admin process. And because we've documented the steps in the correct order and the appropriate time they should be taken, we tend to avoid mistakes.

Wouldn't you prefer to make fewer mistakes and to work more efficiently? To be able to delegate tasks when your business grows? To ensure profitability?

18

Hi, I'm Dan!
How do we sell more?

I've read 40 books on sales and marketing. Most of them talk about stuff that is incomprehensible to the small business owner. I'm always looking for ideas, but often they don't apply to my business.

This is the first of two chapters that will revolutionise your thoughts on sales and marketing. Let's start with sales.

Over the years, people have told me I'm an excellent salesman. Apparently I could sell sawdust to a carpenter. Why is this the case?

There is a considerable amount of science regarding how to sell to people, and it's about appealing to some of our shared human traits. The best salespeople are "non-sales-y," knowledgeable, and understanding of why the customer needs to buy their product or service. Non-sales-y? Well, when we think about sales, we tend to think of that used car salesperson. I know you're picturing someone in your mind right now, the one with all the buzz phrases and smooth talking. But I believe we should never ever see ourselves only as salespeople if we want to sell something. In other words, we should try to be "non-sales-y." Mike Southern, author of the excellent book *Sales on a Beer Mat*, agrees. I've had the good fortune to see him speak, and he was one of the first people to talk sense when it came to sales.

His approach is "Be Liked, Qualify, and Close" (That's the subtitle of his book, by the way.) He's absolutely right.

Be Liked: Don't use stupid sales language; be honest and genuine.

Qualify: Hit the requirements, have the knowledge and the right product, and provide the right price.

Close: Don't forget to ask for the business.

I follow these rules. In my own business, I find it easy to be liked. I'm supportive and caring and I listen to my clients. I love my job and I'm forever grateful – and I show this gratitude. I do simple things like say thank you.

When it comes to "qualifying," I show a good depth of knowledge and use stories about other clients I've worked with to prove I can do the work. I demonstrate slick administrative skills to give the client confidence, and my team reflects the same attributes. When it comes to pricing,

I rarely negotiate. I'm fortunate to have a queue of people wanting to work with me, and I understand my margins.

As for "closing," I always ask the client if they want to come on board or if there's anything stopping them. Doing this becomes an excellent opportunity to overcome initial objections and to shine by handling difficult questions.

I'd like to add something worth noting: I'm not afraid to turn something down when I don't think it suits me or my business. Turning things down is a great skill to acquire; knowing when you don't have the skills is a beneficial trait. We all have to acknowledge that we can't be an expert in everything we do. Take this book, for example. I'm aiming this book at a particular market. I'm not trying to sell it to everyone. I'm trying my best to *be liked*, to *qualify* (by providing backup to my science) and to *close*. Hopefully I've already been doing them all as you've been reading.

How to teach 180 students to sell?

We had 180 keen students who were setting up businesses that needed to make some sales quickly.

We were always learning how to be more successful at getting the students to trade before Christmas. We'd been using some of the principles of lean startup and were looking to make things more efficient. Our industry speakers were part of this plan.

We brought in a guest professional presentation coach to give a lecture to our students on the Graduate Enterprise module. Do note that although our objective was to teach them to sell, we didn't bring in a selling expert. We brought in a presentation expert.

We'd been using Dan Bond for several years but this particular year we arranged to bring him in earlier in the academic year so that he could teach the students how to present themselves before the Christmas trade fair. We wanted him to teach the students how to become sales animals! We thought: What if we could teach them the basics just before they started to trade? It would be a case of utilising marginal gains and following the principles of lean methodologies.

I walked into the lecture theatre and greeted Dan. Though we'd been using Dan for several years, I'd never been able to attend his sessions, so I'd never met him or witnessed what he did. He asked me questions like how many students were present, what courses did they take, what were some examples of the students' business ideas, etc. Then I asked him if he had any slides I needed to load onto the computer. I couldn't wait to see his slides! This man had a client list to die for, and his slides would indeed knock me out.

"No, I don't have any slides."

A presentation coach with no slides?! Little did I know I was about to be schooled in how to give a presentation. "Excuse me, I need to make a start," he said.

"But the lecture doesn't start for 10 minutes."

"Perfect!"

As the students slowly took their seats and entered the lecture theatre, Dan stood almost motionless, observing the students from the front of the room. He was like a wild animal waiting for its prey.

This man was bonkers!

But all of a sudden, a student made eye contact with him. He sprang to life! He waved and shouted at them, "Hi, I'm Dan!" and charged up the lecture theatre stairs. He then sat for a few moments talking to the student. Then he made contact with another student and repeated the same process. At exactly 1:10pm, when the lecture was due to start, he was back at the front, ready to present.

By the way, I should mention that the 1pm lecture slot is the graveyard shift. In winter, the heating is on full blast and everyone has just had lunch. It's not uncommon to find a student asleep at the back.

"Before we start, can we wish Julie a happy birthday! Everybody give her a round of applause," Dan began.

Of course, he had the students' attention the second he started. The students knew he was a guest lecturer, so how could he know their names, let alone the fact it was Julie's birthday? There was more fantastic stuff to come.

"I've just been talking to Tom, who's got a tea business, and he's been struggling to find the right audience for his product," he said.

It was only at this point he decided to say more about himself.

"I'm here today to teach you how to present yourself and sell in the best possible way."

He took advantage of everything he'd just learned from everyone he'd spoken to and crafted his lecture around that information. Even the questions he had asked me before he started were woven into his presentation. He used my name and mentioned that I had my own business.

Here's where I need to stop for a moment and explain something.

I realised after Dan's lecture that he had based it on Robert Cialdini's 1984 book *Influence: The Psychology of Persuasion*. This book outlines his "Six Principles of Human Persuasion" and it continues to be valid today. Cialdini later added a 7th principle. For the purposes of this chapter, I will refer to these principles.

They are:

1. Being Liked
2. Reciprocity
3. Scarcity
4. Authority

5. Commitment and Consistency
6. Consensus (social proof)
7. Unity (this is the one Cialdini added later)

Let's look at Dan's lecture with these principles in mind:

He was immediately *liked*. From the outset, he had the students in the palm of his hand. I'd never seen a lecture theatre so full of engaged students. His presentation was genius; he used familiar ground throughout. He used different tones of voice, he was animated, and he used lots of funny jokes.

He told them about how he worked with important CEOs and politicians to improve their presentation skills. In doing so, he gave himself *authority*. Furthermore, he explained to the students the importance of authority and why he'd spent time getting to know the students at the start of the lecture.

He discussed how charities give out free pens in order to create a sense of *reciprocity*: if you give something to someone, they will want to give you something back. So guess what all the students had on their trade stands at the Christmas market - a pot of free sweets. If you've ever done a trade fair yourself you might have given away freebies, but have you ever asked yourself why? Reciprocity.

Dan explained discounting and deadlines and how this creates *scarcity*. I encountered this recently when I was given a quote for a kitchen renovation. The salesman said,

"There's a 50% discount at the moment but it ends next week, the price will go up at that point. Plus, once you pay the deposit, you lock in the material prices." An excellent example of scarcity. Just look at what happened before the COVID lockdown. When McDonalds was going to close its doors, there were queues for miles. It was *scarcity* in action!

As for *consensus* or *social proof,* some students adorned their trade fair booths with framed testimonials.

The Christmas market following Dan's talk was wonderful because he had given the students a lot of tips about how to effectively present at a trade stand. The tips reflected Cialdini's seven principles:

- Don't stand behind the table, as the customer may feel less invited to approach. Stand in front so you can mingle and be welcoming, rather than foreboding. This is about *being liked.*

- Create a "Trade Fair Only Special Offer!" to create *scarcity.*

- Don't put too many people on the trade stand at once because they will tend to get bored. Split up the work so everyone is fresh and engaged. Too many people on the stand can also make it seem unapproachable. Avoid clutter; make it neat & tidy. Wear a uniform. Provide transparent pricing. These simple examples show *consistency and commitment* because they demonstrate that the staff members are on the same page with each other and that all customers will receive the same price and service offering. And if the staff aren't bored it will lead to them to be more committed to every customer interaction. Even wearing uniforms makes it clear to your potential customers that the staff are members of the team, rather than just random people visiting the trade show. In general, the brain uses a method of shortcutting in order to reduce the number of decisions it needs to make. Therefore, keeping things simple will make it easier for your customer or client to make a decision about buying. It's why the principles of cross selling work – if they have a desire to buy from you but the product isn't the right one, a cross sell can work well.

🜨 Prepare some testimonials, screenshots of Google Reviews, or social media posts to provide *social proof*. Most importantly, have a demonstration of your product. I had a student group one year selling selfie sticks (remember when they were all the rage?). They booked a trade stand at the Metro Centre, the North East's biggest shopping centre. When I checked on them, I asked, "How many have you sold?" "None!" I was with my little boy, who was 3 at the time. So I took one out of the box and started taking photos. Within a minute, someone was buying one. I came back an hour later and they were sold out. The product is no use in a box, and it was a great example of *social proof* when potential customers could witness me using one. I represented a person just like them, so when they saw someone like them using the product they could envision themselves using it. The product became socially acceptable to own.

- Smile and say good morning to everyone who passes. Thank people for looking at the products. Ask people if they need help. In other words, *be liked*. And when you are asked to show your product, make sure you are very knowledgeable about it, to create a sense of *authority*.

- Never eat on the trade stand. I walk around many trade fairs and I hate seeing this – it looks rubbish. You won't be *liked* and you don't look like an *authority*.

How do I build Cialdini's principles into our sales strategy?

Reciprocity

The first way I do this is by giving everyone one free hour of consultation with my organisation. This isn't some sales tactic but a meeting about giving solid advice.

A client comes to me and tells me, "I'm in a pickle with HMRC. My business is in dire straits and I don't have enough money to feed the family." I reply, "Come and have an hour with me and let me see if I can help." Free of charge. Why? It's *reciprocity*. That said, I am careful with this type of reciprocity. I must genuinely want to help, and I must be prepared to give my time away for nothing. To me, time is one of the most valuable things I can give someone.

I try to go out of my way to help someone every day. If I can help, then at some point in the future they will try to repay me. After all my years in business, I'm reaping this daily. I might have to wait 5 years, but people do eventually come to find me.

Scarcity

We're not desperate for work, so I tend not to need to negotiate or discount. Sometimes we set deadlines for taking on tax return clients, so this can encourage people to come on board. The deadlines generate scarcity.

Authority

One of the reasons I've written this book is to build authority. (Hopefully people will read it!) Furthermore, I teach at a university, I'm already published in entrepreneurship, and I have a long list of happy clients who bolster my authority through their positive word-of-mouth.

Commitment and Consistency

We have to deliver on time and with a consistent level of service. For my business, this is about processes. No one should be treated differently; everyone should get the same level of service and attention no matter who they are. The standard of work needs to be excellent, as do our standards of communication. I have a service business so this is extremely important. Finally, at the end of each week, we make a list of all the client proposals sent that haven't been closed. We ring them up – follow-ups are all-important.

They show consistency and give you another opportunity to reflect your authority.

Consensus (Social Proof)

We try to encourage clients to make referrals. We specifically ask clients to suggest us to other customers and to leave reviews about their experience with us. For more about this type of strategy, I recommend Ken Blanchard's terrific 1993 book *Raving Fans*. (More on this book in an upcoming chapter.)

Be Liked

My primary method of being liked is to get to know the client by asking lots of questions and learning about the problems they face. I listen carefully, I take notes, and I remember. And because I understand personality types I am very adept at presenting information in ways that clients can relate to. People always want to work with people who seem to be the same as they are. Plus, if I've ticked all the boxes for the other 6 principles of human persuasion, then being liked comes relatively easily. That all said, there can be exceptions. One client of mine once told me that the deciding factor for working with me was my star sign!

Unity

This is about reminding your target audience that they are part of a community. If you see people you consider to be the same as you using a product or service, you are more likely to feel like part of that group. Remember the selfie sticks? In addition to providing social proof, that story also exemplifies the principle of unity: potential customers who use the selfie sticks all become members of the selfie stick gang! Lego is a similar example of this type of unity building. We see other children playing with Lego and we want to become a part of that experience. The Lego company has done a tremendous job of creating an entire community whose members all want to interact and stay connected. They even play with Lego together in the company's stores! There is more on how my own business utilises the principle of unity in the next chapter.

Asking for business

One of the most important skills I've ever acquired regarding selling to people is to ask for their business.

You can say things like:

- I'd really like to win your business and work with you. Is there anything I can do to help you feel comfortable with coming on board?
- Have I answered all your questions?
- Is there anything stopping you from working with me?

Just remember your answers have to be true.

I pinched the idea of "asking" from working with a charity. Someone I knew worked for a charity, and they told me about a concept called "The Ask." It included the idea that someone would be specifically designated as the "asker" before a pitch presentation to a corporate sponsor. In other words, a careful plan was created in advance for someone to *directly* ask for the money. Asking for things should be a part of your business strategy.

In general, it's surprising in business how few people don't ask for the work.

If you don't ultimately win a contract, ask the person if they'd be willing to make an introduction to any of their other business contacts. It's human nature that we don't like to say "no" – we tend to want to help. It's just a different type of "ask." It's just about psychology, and in this case it's called the Ben Franklin effect. I'll leave it up to you to read up on that one!

Emotional Investment

There is a fascinating study from 2003 that was conducted by Naomi Eisenberger. The study shows that emotional pain creates the same chemical reaction in the brain as the one caused by physical pain. I mention this study because I believe it proves the important point that emotional pain is nothing to take lightly. As business people we have a deep emotional investment in our businesses, so it's not surprising how hurt we can feel after rejection or failure. In my dealings with other business people and clients, I try not to inflict this hurt on others. In fact, I aim to reduce the amount of hurt and pain. In sales, keep an eye out for the issues and obstacles that cause such negative feelings. If you can overcome them by listening and asking the right questions, a potential client or colleague will likely be much more inclined to work with you.

I hope all this has given you some ideas to apply to your sales processes and reveals a few answers behind why we use various sales techniques.

19

Herman "The German"
How do we appeal to more people

If science is defined as the discovery of the world via experimentation, then marketing is the best example of science happening in business. People confuse marketing with being an art form because it involves the process of storytelling. However, marketing is more about testing hypotheses. In our modern business world, it has never been easier to see marketing as a science. We have data at our fingertips and web technologies with tracking tools. It's easy to measure the results of our marketing experiments and to see if our hypotheses work.

I'll start with a story about marketing.

In 2004 I set up a web development business with my friend Dom. We'd had a good run at the business while at university with three other friends, and Dom and I decided to keep it going after we left university.

Dom set about creating a professional website to kick off our "proper" company. This was before the days of pre-made website templates, so bespoke designed websites took ages. After two weeks of hard graft Dom had finished the website. We proudly put it live and I emailed everyone I knew to tell them about it.

Within a few hours we had an enquiry. Someone had filled out the website contact form. Herman Ogmire, the owner of a sausage factory making high end German sausages, had contacted us. He wanted to branch out into e-commerce. I was so excited! This marketing stuff was already working! A client with a proper business and likely a proper budget!

I picked up the office landline straight away – there was no time to waste! Herman answered the phone with a thick German accent. I thanked him for filling in our contact form. I was then confronted with uncontrollable laughter from the other end of the phone. It was my best friend Ben playing a prank on me! I really should have seen the hallmarks.

It was an important lesson for two reasons.

First, traffic (whether web or physical) will not just arrive at your door. Our new website didn't attract anyone other than the people we already knew.

Second, despite the practical joke, a conversation had been started.

"Are you all up and running then? What sort of clients are you looking for?" Ben asked.

"We're looking for businesses who want to enter the web world with updated websites and graphic design work," I explained.

The conversation went on and I told him all sorts of things about how technology had moved on. I explained what businesses could now do in terms of online advertising and that there was some really powerful tech that businesses could utilise for their marketing.

"I'll ring my dad and tell him what you've just told me. His business will need some help as their website is fairly basic," said Ben.

Within a week I got a call from Ben's dad. He told me he needed a new website and asked to have a meeting. So off Dom and I went to the meeting, a few pre-prepared, speculative designs in hand. One of these designs was a more modern, edgy, and up-to-date logo. Ben's dad hadn't considered a logo redesign but he was quite taken with what we had done. We told him how the world was moving on and how the new brand would sit better in the marketplace.

Dom and I left the meeting with a contract for graphic design, print, and web work. We did a lot of work for Ben's dad in the future – over the first few years of our business it generated about 30% of our turnover.

This experience, including the practical joke, taught me something that I didn't realise until many years later. Why had we won the contract in the first place?

We need people who will execute, we need people who will deliver on promises we make.
Seth Godin

Seth Godin was appointed to the American Marketing Association's Marketing Hall of Fame in 2018. He's written a fair few books on the subject, so he's a good role model for this chapter's discussion of marketing. His quote makes the crucial point that marketing is about people. I think we can easily forget this fact. My introduction to Ben's dad was, in effect, marketing. And, as Godin states, Dom and I also had to make good on the promises we made and to effectively deliver our services.

But this isn't the whole story. Don't worry, answers are around the corner.

The Problem with Marketing

A client told me they had spent £5,000 on a marketing campaign but the phone remained silent. Their marketing consultant informed them that they were now aware of what didn't work, and they could focus the next £5,000 on a different method of marketing. The client asked me whether it was going to be worth it to gamble another £5,000 on marketing.

Marketing is like roulette at the casino. You undertake an activity and most of the time you lose. It's that 80/20 rule coming back to bite us again: 80% of your clients will come from 20% of your marketing spend.

But there is a message for us scientists here: marketing is about experimentation (though maybe not always to the degree of £5,000).

When I changed careers from web development to accountancy, I needed to draw on all my experience in order to create a marketing plan which would truly work. However, I realised that getting people to buy from an accountancy business was going to be difficult.

Why? Well, in short, it's only when another client-accountant relationship breaks down somewhere else that an accountant gets the opportunity to win new work. It's rarely a question of price.

As an accountant you are in the inner circle of trust for your clients, because everything in our lives revolves around money. Getting a divorce, having a baby, buying a house – all these things usually require important financial calculations. Even dealing with death or the potential of death requires our financial affairs to be organised. It's a tremendous responsibility and privilege to have such a relationship with a client.

So the bottom line is that people don't move accountants unless they are unhappy or the accountant is retiring. I am reminded of an example with one of our clients: her previous accountant retired and had left the accounts in a bit of a mess. When I asked her about the situation, she said, "He was such a nice guy and when I called him he always had time for me. We loved working with him." Bizarre! Although the work was poor, she still liked him. How do you overcome that sort of situation?

Thus, when it came to marketing, I needed to create something that was going to be killer!

The Secret Level – Education

Honestly, for a long time, I hadn't really thought about the science of marketing. However, I have discovered that you need to add a secret level to your marketing! Shhhhhhh! (I'm telling you this because I clearly like you for reading my book.)

I've deliberately placed this chapter to follow my discussion on how to sell, the one where I introduced Cialdini's 7 principles of human persuasion. It's important to build the 7 principles into your marketing strategies and your sales for the marketing to succeed. Once you've done that we can start to apply some tools and techniques.

Over the years I've tried all sorts of different things, from letters, email newsletters, cold calling, and trade fairs. Sometimes they worked and sometimes they didn't. Why did I get enquiries on some occasions and on other times not?

I realised that what I was trying to do was to go from enquiry directly to sale. But it dawned on me that the times when I won the client was when I was educating people in between those two stages! With my best friend all those years ago I had educated him about the digital space, and that education led to an introduction. I then won the contract with Ben's dad because we'd educated him about the importance of good design and usability.

Something else I learned was that I won work after being a speaker at events. Looking back to our friend Robert Cialdini and his 7 Principles of Human Persuasion, it was clear that being a speaker gave me *authority*. In my web development business we held seminars for clients during which I'd educate them on various things such as how to do their own SEO (Search Engine Optimisation), how to interpret analytics, how facebook ads work, etc. We charged people to attend these seminars and it resulted in new clients. I believe authority was created because clients would ask themselves, "Imagine how good someone must be at their job if they can charge for a seminar!"

When I moved into the accountancy sector, our marketing changed focus from being about selling directly to giving potential clients the opportunity to learn. This is partly what this book is all about. My reason for writing it is about knowledge sharing. People are often scared about telling people why they are doing something. But that's often what marketing is all about, and we need to stop being afraid of being honest.

We decided to hold free seminars that anyone could attend. They generally were not about accountancy subjects but rather about business knowledge. We geared our marketing ads to target Facebook business page admins in the local area. We used an event system to register tickets and we harvested email addresses to create a list for future events. It was a slow start to the seminars but as time went on we found something amazing was happening.

The people who did come to the seminars picked up invaluable knowledge they could apply in their businesses. They left the seminars better supported and feeling valued. This created *reciprocity* as we'd given away something for free to our attendees and they wanted to give something back. So these people started talking about the great events my business was putting on and the enquiries flowed in. We also noticed that even before we'd deliver the seminar, we'd be on people's minds. The phone was ringing even before we actually did the seminar.

By delivering the seminars I positioned myself in a place of authority and gave myself and my business the chance to *be liked* by people. Furthermore, we created an element of *unity* as our clients began to feel like a part of a meaningful community.

When the 2020 COVID pandemic hit, our options for delivering face to face seminars looked to become quite difficult. My colleague and friend Nasser had been the driving force behind getting the seminars off the ground and, being the clever chap he is, he had another great idea. "Let's open up your diary and offer everyone some free advice about the available government COVID support."

So that's what we did! We used the same facebook advertising method but with an online appointment booking system where anyone could book a 20 minute phone call. Over the course of two weeks I made around 70 phone calls and initiated over 50 messenger conversations. Our approach wasn't one of sales, it was simply one of assistance. Of course I hoped it might lead to some work in the long run, but the principal focus was to help. We won five new clients as a result of the calls and conversations. I had people say to me during the calls that they didn't want a new accountant, they just needed help. Interesting that they were ringing me rather than their own accountant! Regardless of their situation, I was equally helpful to everyone.

If you are prepared to incorporate an education step then powerful results can be achieved. My objective is always for people to simply gain some knowledge – and my understanding of science tells me the benefits will always follow.

Communication

The next part of your plan is communication. People pump out information onto business social media accounts but they forget something critical. They're not the BBC! You can't just broadcast information and expect people to receive it.

When you pick up the telephone and have a conversation, it's two-way – we take turns to talk. Yet, when we take to social media we tend to think that one-way will be enough. When we use social media we need to have the same mantra of two-way communication. Why not start a conversation by asking a question rather than just pumping

217

out news or advertising. You have to be interesting and you can only be interesting if you share genuine content.

Rather than saying "Special offer - get 20% off on your next course on staff management" say "Who has problems with staff lateness?". Start a conversation first and offer some free advice. Build trust, authority, and become liked then you can share your paid content later.

I had the great fortune to see a local marketer named John McRae speak. He'd created a great concept in which he utilised a mix of stand up comedy and marketing advice. Behind his funny stories was a brilliant idea. One of the concepts John illustrated was the principle of a **unique selling benefit.** Rather than using lots of unique selling points, boil it down to the single reason someone will use your business. Just one reason! It makes it easy to communicate and it sells the business in one line.

Here's an example: let's look at my fantastic local insurance broker. I could buy the same policy £50 cheaper if I bought it online, so why do I use my broker? Well, when I call them the phone is answered after 3 rings, by either Jenn or Lucy. They know my name; they remember me. I don't have to sit in a long queue of people, and they care about me being covered correctly. When I forget to renew they ring me (yes, they actually use a telephone and ring me). If I was dealing with a national organisation I would wait on average 15 minutes for the call to be answered and the service would usually be below average.

If you ask this small insurance broker about their unique selling points, they'll tell you lots of things about their cover, being local, and having access to the entire insurance marketplace. Yet, to me, their unique selling benefit is having a real human connection with their clients.

Another aspect of communication is when our subconscious makes decisions. We might not think that our innate senses play a part in business but the brain uses the senses to decide if it is attracted to something. These senses have been studied in great detail and they all feed into the decision making process. More importantly, they can be part of our communication. When we walk into a business the first thing we do is see and smell. If it smells of rotten cabbage then it's going to be a major turn off. Whether we like it or not the brain is making subconscious decisions. First impressions count!

So, make sure your website is uncluttered and your designs look professional. The coffee cups aren't chipped. The coffee you serve tastes nice. Side note: the quality of the coffee can be a make or break for me!

In short, when it comes to communication, be well organised, neat, and tidy. Make sure you are actually communicating with your audience, and find that unique selling benefit.

Service Level

Did you know delivering merely satisfactory service isn't good enough?

Think about that for a minute. Of course, if we have a bad experience we'll tell other people about it, it's human nature. And if something is exceptional then we're likely to tell everyone! But where does satisfactory service fit in? Well, when people get merely satisfactory service, they don't tell anyone. So how do we be more than merely satisfactory? I believe the fundamentals of customer service are really easy to understand and usually quite simple to implement.

When you do brilliant things for your clients/customers they become "raving fans." In other words, brand advocates. They generate word of mouth referrals, which are the gold dust of businesses. My own business spends less than £100 on marketing each month simply because we have raving fans.

Ken Blanchard coined this term in his great 1993 book *Raving Fans*. Raving fans are people, usually (but not always) your clients, who will shout down anyone who uses a competitor's service over the one that your business offers. Think about Apple iPhone users – what happens the moment someone pulls out their inferior Android phone? Or, god forbid, they complain about their Android phone not working? I can already hear myself saying, "I don't have that problem with my iPhone." See, I'm an Apple raving fan!

I've been a huge fan of Michael Heppell's books over the years, especially *How to be Brilliant*. Michael doesn't talk about complex formulas but rather about finding ways to take an experience from being merely satisfactory to being brilliant. I'd recommend you read a couple of his books as they are full of ideas to give you an edge.

A simple example from my own business is that when we receive a client referral I always write a note to the client to thank them. Why? Because they have trusted me with information about a business contact or personal friend. I first express my gratitude and then express my confidence that we'll wow the referral with an excellent level of service. If you say thank you to a client, you have to mean it.

Finding ways of delivering better than average service is one of the strongest marketing tools out there.

Be Realistic and Keep it Simple

Marketing is like a triathlon. (Just when you thought I'd finished my triathlon stories!)

A triathlon race is the culminating event I aim to complete, but the preparation (at least for me) starts months before. It involves turbo training, interval running sessions, strength & conditioning, and swimming at both the club and in rivers and lakes. It's a massive ask of my body, so I must prepare.

So what has triathlon got to do with marketing?

When I started marketing my book, I didn't expect overnight success as I see marketing as a triathlon. The marketing planning started five months before the book launch date, and I actively started marketing the book 80 days before the release date. Everything culminates in the book launch, but the preparation takes place well in advance.

When I undertake my triathlon training, I split it into five phases, and I've done the same for this book:

Phase 1: Acclimatisation – preparing the body for training

For marketing my book, this compares to the planning phase that started about five months prior. I used a Trello board to create a project plan that included all the critical marketing milestones. I essentially brainstormed all the activities I needed to do to get the word out there about my little book project.

Phase 2: Base Phase – building endurance in all three sports

When it came to my book and its marketing I decided to go for a pre-launch. I realised I needed to start building a tribe, otherwise I'd have no following when I published. Therefore, I needed to warm up into my marketing with some emails to existing clients and friends. I also held a free webinar, and I networked with existing contacts. These activities represented the slow and steady build-up of customers before the main book launch in the same way my months of triathlon training built up my endurance before the race.

Phase 3: Build Phase – increase volume and types of activity

I've planned a big marketing splash when the book is available to order and be delivered. I'll ask my initial pre-order customers to leave reviews to build some authority. I've already been booked as a speaker for an event a few months after the book launch. I'll enter a few book competitions, start an online ads campaign, do more webinars to take advantage of my education marketing, and of course do some PR.

Phase 4: Peak Phase – hit maximum mileage

During this phase, everything is happening at once and I should start to see the book sales being generated from word of mouth. I'll be paying attention to all the data and analytics to find out which of our marketing experiments are working the best. We can then refocus if necessary.

Phase 5: Tapper phase – let your body recover and reduce volume

The book may be a success, who knows? But by the time I reach this last phase I've given it my best shot, whether it results in success or failure. We will have generated educational video material during the other phases that will be applied to our online ads formula, and we'll do something they call "sell through." This means the book should start to gain traction and generate sales through word of mouth without very much active marketing.

My final word

Just remember to apply science when you can. Use the 7 principles, use education as a tool, think about communication, boost customer service, and view marketing as a triathlon, not a sprint.

Modern marketing with technology makes it easy to measure performance and undertake experiments. But don't be disheartened if a project gets off to a slow start. When I run a seminar I might only have 30 people signed up. Some people might think this is low, but I think, "Brilliant, this is 30 people I've never met before and who didn't know about my book project." Not only that, they are contacts where I might be able to get value in the future. You might be disheartened by early performance numbers, but don't be. It takes time, so don't give up.

Just remember that quote from Seth Godin: if you promise something in marketing, make sure your people can keep the promise and deliver.

20

Down at the Police Station
Time: stop thinking about work as a 9-5

Is time a science? I've mentioned the word "time" 234 times in this book, so it must be important. I'm assured that time is the fourth dimension. I've tried to read Stephen Hawking's book, but it's beyond me.

I know one thing for sure about time. It's the one commodity I can't buy more of.

The subject of time might be challenging to justify in my book. The related themes of regret, money, time, and happiness are very much up for discussion. Psychologists have long been publishing papers about the correlation between money and happiness.

Imagine for a moment that you turn off the alarm and decide to have a lie-in. It's a beautiful day and you decide against the opportunity to meet up with some friends or go for a walk. Later that day, you wish you had spent your time differently.

You're experiencing the emotion of regret.

We learn about the emotion of regret as children and, according to some research, it's pretty helpful for children to experience regret as it leads them to better decision-making. Furthermore, when children do ultimately receive rewards and feel success, their gratification is greater if they have already experienced regret.

I sometimes feel slightly resentful about how I spent my 20s. In hindsight (isn't that a wonderful thing), I regret having a poor work-life balance and not having enough money while starting my business. Yet I wonder if the findings of the study would be the same for adults. I still regret missed opportunities from earlier in my life, but the regret seems to diminish if I have the chance to do them now.

We set goals from early in our lives, but as we age, I think something has to give in terms of achieving some of them. We have to choose to give time to some things over others, and it's hard to avoid the regret of missing some potential aspects to our lives.

I questioned one person in my life who I knew had some regrets, someone who had built a hugely successful business and raised a child as a single parent. I was curious about how they felt about time and regrets. What role did money play in their ability to achieve happiness?

Time & Regrets

The person I'm talking about is my mum. I couldn't write a book without telling a story about her. I think her story relates some important lessons about how we spend time and money.

When my mum set up her law firm, I was just four years old. She was the first female solicitor in town, and a single parent to boot. Years later one of the other local solicitors told me that she was "Five foot of shit and grit." I hope that allows you to form an immediate picture of her! Let's just say she's a ferocious character.

In the early stages of her business she needed to ensure a constant income, so she took on the role of duty solicitor. Imagine a police show on TV where the criminal declares, "I want a lawyer!" It was my mum getting that call. It all looks glamorous on TV, but the reality is that someone has drunk 15 pints of lager, gotten blind drunk, had a fight, and ended up getting arrested.

I remember her getting the calls to come down to the police station in the evening. "Tell them I'll come down when they've slept it off," she'd tell the police officer. Saturday morning was usually when the exciting stuff started to happen. It was either the magistrate court appointments or police interviews for those detained after a Friday night of drunken fighting. The detainees needed to be interviewed so very sensibly they asked for the duty solicitor. To their good fortune, the five foot of shit and grit came to their aid.

But, as a single parent, she didn't always have childcare, so off we both went to the police station. It was connected to the court, as it happens, so it was all very convenient from a childcare perspective. I was plopped on a seat next to the desk sergeant, where I could watch the comings and goings through the police station door while doing my colouring. At the same time, my mum would be representing the accused in an interview room or in the courtroom. It was great! I met loads of coppers, and they took me to the mess for a glass of milk or a biscuit, sometimes both!

Many of these strange experiences led me to discover that police officers are normal people – people who are there to help and who should never be feared. Of course, taking a child down to the police station would never be allowed these days. But what an experience.

It didn't stop there. My early childhood saw me going to networking events, Law Society dinners, and occasionally the prison. I was even stuffed under the desk at the court on one occasion. It was all quite an adventure, and it was the start of my education about how society works. One particular experience comes to mind from when I was about eight years old. As my mum and I were driving through town, we passed a chap in a wheelchair. My mum pointed him out to me and said, "He's a crime wave on wheels." I'd never imagined someone could use a disability to profit from crime. It seemed unfathomable to me at the time.

I started to form a value system based on what I saw.

The creation of my values came into focus when a mother and young son arrived at our home. She was one of my mum's clients and the visit was entirely against the rules. My mum was a member of the children's panel, a scheme whereby solicitors represent and make legal decisions for children who are going through their darkest hour of need. When I asked why these people were at our house my mum answered, "I'm worried her husband might kill them." I then realised that while something can be against the rules, you can always choose to do what is right – it's a question of values.

The adventures with my mum ended when she started earning enough to send me to a private school. It was the advantage of school on Saturday morning, sports matches in the afternoon, and school until 6 pm. My mum had been despairing because I was way behind with my reading and writing skills and she lacked the time to help me. Private school, in her eyes, was the answer. It wasn't about status, but simply about the practical reality that she couldn't do everything.

I was brought up by a busy single parent, and I'm an only child. As I got older, I started to take more responsibility. I was, in effect, the man of the house. I developed a sense of maturity while quite young. For example, one day there was a note and some money on the kitchen table. I was required to provide some evening meals. After beans on toast the first night, my mum told me I should take a look at the cookbooks. A quick look at the bookshelf introduced me to Rick Stein. I loved eating fish, so I walked to Tesco, and for that evening's meal I served plaice fillets.

I became independent out of necessity. By my later teenage years I was cooking, doing the garden, organising plumbers, and helping with jobs around the house. I had gained a sense of responsibility and purpose.

"Did you feel neglected as a child?" my mum asked me recently. Maybe she was feeling pangs of remorse that she didn't have enough time for me growing up. But my answer was no. I never felt neglected, and I have a great relationship with my mum. And how I was brought up made me the man I am today.

So why am I talking about this weird upbringing? It's all about time, and how we can't get it back and how we must choose what we do with it. The story of my mum is one of a single parent trying to do everything yet not always being able to find the time to do so.

I think it's hard to try to have everything while also achieving a sense of balance. Before you read on, I want to mention that while my mum was short on time, there were many things she did to build a connection with me. When she needed to go to the prison, we spent the travel time together catching up. We sat together at those Law Society dinners. When I cooked the evening meals, she'd be there to eat them with me. She was wise with her time and maximised the moments she could afford to spend with me.

I know that she's immensely proud of my well-rounded personality and of the man I've become. Her general mantra in life is that anyone can achieve anything and that opportunities should be available for everyone. I suppose my upbringing reflected this mantra – she wouldn't be held back as a woman, a solicitor, or a single parent.

What have I learned?

My experiences growing up have certainly affected me as a parent. I want more time with my children than my mum had with me. Yet will that mean they don't learn what I learned?

I want you to think about time. How do you view it? I want you to value your time and to put a price on it. That's more important than anything else. If you feel like you've wasted time, don't regret it. Learn from it. As a business owner, I have a choice. How much time do I spend on my business, my family, and my personal activities? It is essential for health and well-being to get this balance right. Why do I feel slightly resentful about how I spent my 20s? I regret not having a good work-life balance. But that regret shouldn't stop me from doing things differently now and in the future.

After a discussion with my wife in 2013, I decided to go to a 4-day week. An Icelandic research paper that had recently hit the headlines showed me how effective this strategy could be. This was back when our first son was 18 months old and we'd just lost a staff member. Yet my answer was to work less! Even better, I convinced my wife to work more (4 days per week instead of 3). This would mean we'd both be on a 4-day week.

The strategy has worked wonderfully over the years! Before my kids were in school, I took them swimming and out on adventures, and I had time to do more stuff for my family. Basic stuff like doing the shopping and getting things organised.

When my children both started school I still had no intention of going back to work full time (and neither did my wife, for that matter). We met friends for bike rides and runs, I still did the shopping, and I still fit in the swimming lessons. We take our days off on different days so that the children can have a full day with at least one of their parents two days out of five. It also means we have one less day of after school care to pay for.

I don't want to tell you I'm a master of everything. On every day off, I do some element of work. There is no exception. To work on your day off!? Yes, I do some aspects of work even on days off. I'll send quick email responses, and if I'm in the car driving somewhere I'll make some calls.

There's a bit of an element of illusion here. Just because someone contacts me doesn't mean I have to pick up the phone or read an email or text. But if I'm driving to do some shopping, then sure, I'll take the call. Or I'll ring someone back during some dead time. People will wait! But, and this is a big but, if someone rings me or leaves a message, I always get back to them, no exception.

I have realised that I love to work. It's something I need in my life, but it's also something that has to work for me. I don't view my work as just 9-5. I've considered how I want to spend my time, and I suggest you should consider the same thing.

Do I do less work?

As a result of my 4 day work week, I've become more efficient and focused with how I approach my work. I look for quick wins. Templates of emails, automation, AI, and just being generally intelligent about my time. Being focused is a massive part of my life and means I tend to tackle important projects head on. It can still be a challenge to decide which of the many projects come first!

You always have a choice as a business owner. Do you spend more time doing something yourself or do you hire someone to do it for you? How much is time with your family worth?

For me, employing people is an exchange of time. I buy time from them in the hope that I can leverage that now-available time to make more money. Sounds so simple, yes?!

When the business grew and life started to become too hectic, I analysed how much time I spent organising meetings. It was incredible! So I hired a personal assistant (PA). This PA had lived and worked in London and had moved north when she had children. She'd taken a career break, but now her children were all starting school and she was looking for work. She was a brilliant hire. She had loads of experience and knew the role of being a PA. I learned loads from how she approached things – I realised I didn't know everything after all! The point I'm making is that I exchanged money to get my time back.

I have no regrets about what I accomplished in my thirties. And I'm not even talking about work. I'm talking about how much time I spent with my children, my French language learning, becoming a triathlete, writing this book, lecturing, and taking trips in my campervan. I've travelled all over the UK in my camper van going to triathlon events and my kids usually come with me. I've tried to do everything I can to make my wife happy, including encouraging her to get into running and cycling, two sports she now loves.

What about Money?

Does money make you happy? There's no question that money and time have a complicated relationship. Many journal articles discuss this relationship but their findings can be very contradictory.

I'd like to mention one particular journal article published in 2016 by Cassie Mogilner and Michael Norton titled "Time, money and happiness." It draws on the reams of other articles people have written about the same subject. The article suggests that once basic needs are met, more money doesn't increase someone's happiness. Yes, that's right – it *doesn't*. That's because people often spend money on meaningless products. The article argues that a cup of fancy coffee every morning doesn't improve people's happiness. It goes on to suggest that when people use their money to have *experiences* their happiness is more likely to be positively impacted.

Personally, I try to do exactly this. When I buy products, I do so to further enhance an experience – a wetsuit for triathlon, equipment for rock climbing, a campervan for family travel. All these products allow me to have the best possible experience. A swim in a cold river might not be your idea of fun, but for me it's a unique and positive experience. I can't do it without a wetsuit (well I could, but I don't really want to), so the wetsuit makes the experience more enjoyable.

The point is this: I search out experiences, not just meaningless stuff. Those who know me will attest that I have a terrible wardrobe, wear a cheap hairstyle, and don't drive a fancy car (although I do drive a fancy campervan). When you explore my house, you find the things that make my experiences better. You find the paddle board, a carbon road bike, mountaineering gear, etc.

Mogilner and Norton's article also discusses the effects of spending money on others. It shows that when you spend money on someone else, you increase your happiness. My mother is a great example. When she finally had some money to spend, she spent it on giving me a private education. Enabling me to have experiences was a priority for her. I got the chance to try many extracurricular activities and get extra help with my dyslexia. This was great for me, but it was even better for her. Spending her money to give me these experiences made her happier. She loved knowing that I was doing wonderful things and having a less challenging time in school. When I asked my mum how she felt about paying for my private education, she said it was the best money she'd ever spent.

I think the focus of life must be on time, not money. (This is something else the article by Mogilner and Norton summarises really well. Give it a read for more info.) Internet search trends show that more people search for answers about money than about time. But our lives are finite, so our focus should be on time.

Here's a small example. Recently, my dishwasher broke. It was £20 for next-day delivery or eight days for free delivery. Which do you think I chose? We were without a dishwasher for 24 hours and it took 45 minutes to wash the dishes. One solution required the spending of money, but the most crucial factor in my decision was related to saving time. Never has £20 been better spent.

I want you to consider how you spend time (not money). If we devote time to others, we can gain greater happiness. I have never regretted the time I spent teaching someone on my team or at the university. Until I started writing the book, it had never crossed my mind that spending time with others brings me great happiness. I'm hoping that when you read this book, you'll feel you spent the time wisely. If so, I'll be happy knowing that the time I spent writing it was worth it.

21

Why my GP Surgery is Amazing
An example of many of the concepts in action

I've left this chapter until the end as it brings together many of the subjects I've discussed throughout the book. I actually wrote this chapter first but then realised it needed to be at the end.

I had to see my GP (my least favourite activity) following a bicycle mishap. A conversation during that appointment gave me the final prompt I needed to pick up my laptop and finally write this book. Thanks, Dr. L.

Despite my loathing of going to see medical professionals, I'm still fascinated by medical science. As you've read, there is a vast amount to learn from other industries, and medical processes have often been sources of knowledge. Remember checklists and their powerful impact on operating theatre safety? Isn't it wonderful how we can apply medical and sports research in a different area?

The story of a visit to a GP

The NHS is quite something, isn't it? We have access to free health care, which many countries look at with great envy.

Yet, when it comes to the NHS, everyone seems to have views about how it should work or where it should improve. It's hard to make changes in big organisations. It's like repairing a train while it's still moving. At no point does the NHS completely shut down, though, and thank goodness for that. Someone will come to our aid even if we hurt ourselves on Christmas Day. It's also worth pointing out that there are both good and bad staff members in all organisations – those who are the stars and those who are below par. I've been lucky to meet some shining stars of the NHS who love their work. And I've picked one of these bright stars to make my point.

My own good luck aside, I've noticed something recently: there are a lot of people dissatisfied with their GP surgery. It's not so much about the care they get when they see a medical professional but the demands being made on the system as a whole.

I hear all sorts of complaints: how people waited two weeks for an appointment, how the admin staff got things wrong, how the team wasn't pleasant, how they need to ring up at 8 am for an appointment, or how they simply can't get through on the phone. A quick, very unscientific poll in my office showed that only two people are happy with their particular GP surgeries: my wife Sue and myself, and we share the same GP surgery.

I feel a bit bemused when I listen to people complain because that's not the experience my wife and I have with our GP.

So what makes our GP so great?

Our surgery practice uses an online system for reporting when you have a medical problem, and it can be completed at any time, day or night. After submitting your medical issue through the online form, you can expect to receive a call within 24 hours. In my experience, it usually comes within a few hours. You can, of course, still call them on the phone if you prefer, or if you are not technologically savvy.

The callback you receive always seems to be from an actual GP or nurse practitioner. They determine the next steps based on this call. This is the triage process they use to prioritise who needs the most care. Quite often, one call is all that's required to resolve the concern, but on other occasions the call leads to an appointment. The appointments are usually booked for a time within the next few days. When I get to the surgery, the whole staff is delightful – not just the medical team but also the administrative team. They all appear to be happy at work. I have a skilled eye when it comes to teams and can spot a good team a mile off.

What can we learn?

My biking incident required an appointment, so I ended up in front of one of the practice's partners. I complimented him on how wonderfully organised the practice was and how lovely the team always is.

We began a conversation that lasted 20 minutes (my apologies to the other patients in the waiting room!)

After saying thanks for the positive feedback, the GP told me about something that wasn't going his way. Humility sat there in front of me, which is something I rarely encounter. He was a man after my own heart, not frightened to discuss things that weren't working out. He acknowledged some challenges he'd been able to overcome, yet it seemed to me he was feeling the sometimes isolating consequences of leadership.

Despite his challenges, the doctor was still looking to the future and hoping to improve. He had goals in mind and he had a plan to achieve them.

I asked a few questions about whether he'd read various books and academic resources regarding leadership, processes, goal setting, and staff management. Although he wasn't familiar with this type of stuff, he was clearly doing some of it in his practice already.

I'd seen him at work in the past, and he was a great mentor who used any opportunity to educate. He talked about how he wanted to bring on a junior doctor and shape them into the same value system. He wanted the same ethos that he valued to continue. He didn't accept the merely satisfactory – he always strove for brilliance.

I recognised the man in front of me as an excellent GP, but I also saw he didn't fully realise that he's an even better leader and businessman. His love and passion for his job were evident. He continued to tell me about potentially doing some change management consultancy work in the future in order to help other practices.

I asked him why he was so organised compared to most other practices.

"I realised that if you have a poorly organised practice you get lots of complaints and negativity which you end up constantly battling. That constant battle costs time and energy and keeps us from focusing on making the practice better and more innovative. So we implemented ideas like web systems so we could be more efficient and effective, all with the goal of increasing overall customer satisfaction and decreasing complaints."

A very astute observation: if you don't have to deal with negativity, you can focus on what is essential.

Isn't it interesting that an instinctive leader had found the right path without much research? I wonder if he had known about the material, he might have been able to implement things faster or more successfully. Maybe a conversation for the next visit? I might even send him a copy of this book. I just hope he's happy with what I've written.

A GP practice has to be led and run like a business. There will be some who will read that line and be horrified, but it's true. If a GP surgery wants to deliver the best healthcare, they need the following:

- ❀ Good administration: the ability to competently do the boring stuff like making appointments, sending out letters, issuing prescriptions, sending off lab samples, etc

- ❀ Prioritising / Triage (the medical term): who gets seen first based on the seriousness of the condition

- ❀ Resolution: they need to cure, refer, defer, or signpost to specialist care

- ❀ Allocation of resources: work out what needs to be done, when, and by whom

- ❀ Teamwork: a highly effective team makes the magic happen

Never mind a GP practice – these are the things that need to be achieved in all businesses. Companies can use different names for these things – human resources, project management, product development – but they boil down to the same things.

So, can a GP practice really function like a business, and can it be innovative?

I've talked before about how you solve a problem via the process of innovation, so let me share a useful example from my GP.

My GP has a micro-suction machine for cleaning ears (like a tiny vacuum cleaner but for ears). I once asked him why he had one, as most practices didn't.

"I realised early on in my career that if someone presents with an ear infection, there is likely to be a build-up of junk in the ear canal. You can prescribe antibiotic drops, but without cleaning the ear canal, they just don't get where they need to go. So, the patient ends up in a vicious cycle and likely comes back to me," he said.

Who knew ear cleaning could be so fascinating!? The antibiotics are the cure, but you need to remove the root cause before they can work properly. It's one of those straightforward solutions I keep mentioning. (Though my GP will probably point out that it isn't *that* simple.)

Suppose we delve deeper into the two examples I've given about online appointments/triage and ear cleaning. They provide exciting business lessons because, fundamentally, they involve innovation.

Appointment Book & Triage

The appointment booking and triage system is a process innovation. Within the appointment system, there are a multitude of questions. Clearly someone gave some thought to checklists when designing the system. (Though when I asked my GP if he'd read "The Checklist

Manifesto" or Atul Gawande's journal article, he said he hadn't.)

Like my GP, I cannot remember everything about each client, so I have processes in place. My GP is doing something similar. By asking key questions when booking appointments, they are later able to gather a quick overview of the patient without having to read lots of notes.

One such interesting question they ask is, "Are you taking any medication the practice does not know about?" If you think about all the questions a GP or nurse should ask, they're endless. Yet their online system has allowed them to ensure the right questions are asked at the right time. It might seem innocuous and pointless, but it enables the practice to improve its care.

In all businesses, how we gather information upfront when we onboard our clients is critical, and it is one of the best places to start when considering ways to improve.

It's also about speed. Now, speed can be dangerous in medicine, and patients don't really want to think that their doctors are being too speedy. But it's like my own business – it's all very well having 200 tax returns to complete but I can't do them all in one week. I have to use processes. The same thing happens with the GP and his many patients. Suppose he used a pre-completed checklist that showed all his patients and all their symptoms? That type of efficiency would allow him to allocate patients to medical professionals with the requisite skills and experience.

Another client of mine, a retired GP, told me this:

"In medicine, the common is common."

You can take this principle into medical triage and look to resolve the most common issues over the phone. Again, this is about speed. If 80% of the requests for help involve "the common," you are left with just 20%.

The other aspect of all this is the culture and the team. Everyone must remember that the work that people do must be worthwhile and important. Everyone has to understand this notion. Think again about the cleaner responsible for mopping the floors and cleaning surfaces. In medical practices, their work constitutes effective prevention of infection. The staff responsible for admin serve a similarly important role. They are just as critical to the team as they organise necessary after-care or signpost patients to other services.

Ear Cleaning

Ear infection treatment is a process that changes when you suddenly have the option to manage the condition differently. The cleaning of ears is a process innovation. I know that it might seem strange to think about treatment as a process, but adding a micro-suction machine allows the product (medication in this example) to work and the treatment to succeed.

I've tried to analyse the use of aminoglycoside antibiotic ear drops at a GP practice level (i.e across numerous GP practices) to see if the practice I go to is prescribing less of them. Unfortunately, I wasn't able to get the data I needed, plus I'm not sure I would have gotten a big enough sample. Interestingly, I couldn't lay my hands on any study along these lines. I'd be fascinated to know if ear cleaning results in a decrease of re-infection rates and antibiotic usage. That said, I know from my university teaching experience that each NHS trust seems to guard its information closely, despite them all working for the same organisation.

I don't know enough about the NHS to comment on how they undertake data analysis. But it does make one wonder how solving the root cause of a matter might save time and money. How many other business problems could be solved if we'd simply think about doing some analysis? Not just that, but what if the business had someone skilled enough to act on that analysis and be truly innovative?

Conclusions

As with any good science report, journal, or experiment, we should always finish with a conclusion.

I hope this book has shown you that science is all around us. Science can offer us so many answers to the problems and challenges we face in business – they're just waiting to be found. Remember those childhood days when making a poo smell from a science experiment filled you with joy? You can experience that same joy if you apply science to business.

Fundamentally we are in business because of people. All the concepts I discuss in this book, like psychology, social sciences, usability, and human behavioural science, were dreamed up and devised by people! The all-important data analysis I encourage you to do -- it's simply allowing you to measure the impact of people on your business. And whenever we want to expand our business it means we have to expand our team...our circle of people. I hope this book reminds you to never forget the importance of people.

I suppose the last part of the book contains the ramblings of my busy mind. But maybe busy minds are what science is all about – so let's stay busy thinking, considering, and brainstorming.

Running a business is never straightforward. A client came into the office one day to drop something off and there I was refilling the toilet rolls. "It's hard at the top," she said.

It would appear the tasks of the business owner are endless but remember this: You don't need to be the best at everything. Take some of the ideas from this book and find out where science can help.

Acknowledgements

The end of the book, and just a few words of thanks. My family is releasing a sigh of relief that I didn't pick apart their personality types and use them in case studies. My sister-in-law likes to refer to me as Del Boy, but even after that scathing criticism she doesn't feature. Not even a mention of my mother-in-law, who once told me "Rabbits aren't mammals." Thinking about it now, maybe that is content for a whole other book. But for the moment, you've all escaped!

Onto more serious matters...it's challenging to write an acknowledgements section. I have a contact book of many people who support me daily. There are just too many of you to mention, so I'm sorry if I couldn't fit you in.

So let me start with Sue, my exceptionally long-suffering wife, for supporting my crazy projects. This book has been one of them, and I know you'll be relieved when I've published it. You're often full of self-doubt, but you have skills I don't. I know you sometimes believe you can't live up to your overachieving husband, but you're wrong. You're the balance I so often need in my life, the person who tells me to stop when I need to. I have her drinking beetroot juice before running and somehow doing triathlon racing. I'm hoping this book is proof that I can finish a project.

You don't realise the pain involved in writing a book until you've done so. When I handed over my first draft to Sue, her words were, "My head is battered." Thanks for letting me down gently. Maybe that was payback for the gallons of beetroot juice and other things I've forced you to do. We are still married despite this scathing criticism and hopefully her words have driven me to create a great book.

Thanks to my mum, Catherine Turner. She and I have a great relationship and she has been a great source of knowledge over the years. As a single mother you did everything you could for me growing up, and you've been a real inspiration. When I told her she featured in my book she said, "I hope you've told everyone I believe in equal opportunities for all." It's one of the few projects in my business life I've not shown her, so I hope she's happy with the result.

Thanks to Dr. Joanna Berry, my Young Enterprise Mentor, who helped me when I set up my business at university. You never said no. You always found the time, always came to my aid when things went wrong, and even fed me on occasions. I cannot express how much I appreciate everything you did for me in those early years.

My first year in business as a young enterprise company can't be overlooked, so here's a special mention to my uni mates Ed Gramolt, James Pocock, Andy Devey, and Dom Bennett. We all remember the days when the university bar was the office. Our first client meeting (a dentist) was going so well until James asked for five sugars in his cup of tea. Great memories were made, and you all played an essential role in showing me what a great team looks like.

Thanks to Steve Ball from Northumbria University, who has attempted to rein me in. We've made a formidable team and it has been a joy to learn from you over the last decade. You've given me insight into an academic world that has provided some necessary balance to make a gung-ho entrepreneur think like an academic. Ok, maybe not all the time. I must thank you for those statistics I used in the chapter "The Business of Students."

Thanks to Michael Heppell – you've pushed me into many things I didn't want to do with my little book project. Your books have provided me with much-needed guidance and support. You've been a great friend to my businesses over the years, and I can't wait to see what the future holds. Plus, your excellent "Write that Book" course was the magic dust I needed. I'm sure magic dust is science…maybe we can debate that later.

Thanks to Steven Holmberg, who has done a fantastic job editing the book. I know how hard you worked on getting it all into the best shape possible so thank you. You took my poor English and turned it into something I was proud to publish.

Thanks to Matt Bird, author of *JackFruit Treasure Trap*, for typesetting the book. You've done the invisible work that most don't even realise is there. Those few words of encouragement when you saw the first chapters made me recognise I had created something that might be ok.

Thanks to Alistair Smith from Print & Mail Runner in Newcastle for printing my bookmarks and postcards.

Thanks to Lewis Rickman, my graphic designer, who has done an excellent job with my book cover and logo.

Thanks to Karl Perry, the author of the both shocking and funny *You Only Live Thrice*, for meeting me 1-to-1. I hope I've managed to bottle my enthusiasm and zeal for life as you suggested. You picked me up at a low point in my writing. Someone should write a chapter about that!

Thanks to Chris Race and Keely French, two of my fantastic team members who helped get this book over the line. Chris, you gave me a significant confidence boost to continue the project after reading the initial 50 pages of the book. I think you said, "I read your book sample over the weekend, and I couldn't put it down." Keely has been my PA for about a year – Keely, you help keep me focused even when I'm distracted with things like this book. Plus, you gave me some great feedback during the book's development when I couldn't pull some of the chapters together.

Thanks to my team at Orange Umbrella and Abode Living for being so great to work with on a daily basis. I know I can be infuriating, but I'll always have your back.

I couldn't finish my acknowledgements without a special mention to two other people from outside my world of business.

Thanks to Andy Stevens, my triathlon coach. You've helped me get to a place with my triathlon racing that I never thought possible. You're always patient when my business life requires me to miss sessions. If you ever read this, maybe you'll get a glimpse into my crazy life of consideration and deep thinking. You showed me the power of coaching not just in sport but also in how brilliant people can be the catalyst to help others achieve their goals in life.

Finalement un mot de remerciement. Thanks to Séréna Calgari, my fantastic French tutor. You've helped me more than just helping me learn French. I honestly didn't believe I could learn to speak French. I do think learning French has changed my cognitive ability for the better. Plus, I've read the science around this, so it must be right!

References

Introduction

Waller, J. (2018). Unsexy Business: How 12 entrepreneurs in ordinary businesses achieved extraordinary success and how you can too (1st ed.). Harriman House.

Lupton, E. (2014). Thinking with type: A critical guide for designers, writers, editors, & students. Chronicle Books.

Feisner, E. A. (2006). Colour: How to use colour in art and design. Laurence King Publishing.

O'Connor, Z. (2015). Colour, contrast and gestalt theories of perception: The impact in contemporary visual communications design. Color Research & Application, 40(1), 85-92.

1. Read lots consider carefully

Kiyosaki, R. T. (2022). Rich dad poor dad: What the rich teach their kids about money that the poor and middle class do not! (25th Anniversary ed.). Plata Publishing.

Goldacre, B. (2009). Bad science. Fourth Estate.

Macy, B. (2021). Dopesick: Dealers, doctors and the drug company that addicted america (Reissue ed.). Apollo.

2. What science tells business

Pink, D. H. (2018). Drive: The surprising truth about what motivates us (Main ed.). Canongate.

Pink, D. (2009, July). The puzzle of motivation. www.ted.com. https://www.ted.com/talks/dan_pink_the_puzzle_of_motivation?language=en

Smith, J. (2017). Transforming travel: Realising the potential of sustainable tourism. Cabi.

Study on the re-use of hotel towels: Force of habit saves laundry and cuts pressure on the environment. (n.d.). Www.tuigroup.com. https://www.tuigroup.com/en-en/media/press-releases/2017/2017-08-08-study-on-the-re-use-of-hotel-towels

Glucksberg, S. (1962). The influence of strength of drive on functional fixedness and perceptual recognition. Journal of experimental psychology, 63(1), 36.

3. The Power of the Moon

Tracy, B. (2017). Eat that frog! 21 great ways to stop procrastinating and get more done in less time. Berrett-Koehler Publishers.

Skrynka, J., & Vincent, B. T. (2019). Hunger increases delay discounting of food and non-food rewards. Psychonomic bulletin & review, 26(5), 1729-1737.

Doran, G. T. (1981). There's a SMART way to write management's goals and objectives. Management review, 70(11), 35-36.

Hale, R., & Whitlam, P. (1997). Practical problem solving & decision making: an integrated approach. Kogan Page Publishers.

NHS. (n.d.). Quality, service improvement and redesign (QSIR) tools. NHS choices. Retrieved July 23, 2022, from https://www.england.nhs.uk/sustainableimprovement/qsir-programme/qsir-tools/

4. Have you ever tried drinking a litre of beetroot juice

Murphy, M., Eliot, K., Heuertz, R. M., & Weiss, E. (2012). Whole beetroot consumption acutely improves running performance. Journal of the Academy of Nutrition and Dietetics, 112(4), 548-552.

Daniels, J. (1989). Training Distance Runners. Sport science exchange, 1(11).

McGrath, Mahony, N., Fleming, N., & Donne, B. (2019). Is the FTP test a reliable, reproducible and functional assessment tool in highly-trained athletes?. International Journal of Exercise Science, 12(4), 1334.

University of Tokyo. (2021, March 19). Study shows stronger brain activity after writing on paper than on tablet or smartphone: Unique, complex information in analog methods likely gives brain more details to trigger memory. ScienceDaily. Retrieved July 23, 2022 from www.sciencedaily.com/releases/2021/03/210319080820.htm

5. 80/20 Rules the Roost

Pareto, V. (1964). Cours d'économie politique (Vol. 1). Librairie Droz.

Rober, M. (2015). Best Guess Who Strategy - 96% WIN record using Math. In YouTube. https://www.youtube.com/watch?v=FRlbNOno5VA

6. The Swimmer With One Arm

Locke, E. A., & Latham, G. P. (2006). New directions in goal-setting theory. Current directions in psychological science, 15(5), 265-268.

Heppell, M. (2014). How to be brilliant: change your ways in 90 days! Pearson.

Matthews, G. (2015). Study focuses on strategies for achieving goals, resolutions.

Fogg, B. J. (2019). Tiny habits: The small changes that change everything. Eamon Dolan Books.

7. The Injured Deer

Myers, I. (1962). The Myers Briggs type indicator: Manual. Palo Alto, CA: Consulting Psychologists Press.

Herman, M. (Director). (2008). The boy in the striped pyjamas [Film]. Miramax.

Erikson, T., Pender, M., & Bradbury, R. (2019). Surrounded by idiots : the four types of human behaviour (or, how to understand those who cannot be understood). Vermilion.

Tuckman, B. W. (1965). Developmental sequence in small groups. Psychological bulletin, 63(6), 384.

Belbin, M. (2004). Belbin team roles. Belbin Team Roles.

8. Becoming a clairvoyant

Childress, A. R., & Burns, D. D. (1981). The basics of cognitive therapy. Psychosomatics, 22(12), 1017-1027.

Hammond, J. S., Keeney, R. L., & Raiffa, H. (2006). The hidden traps in decision making. Harvard business review, 84(1), 118.

Aha! + Aaaah: Creative Insight Triggers a Neural Reward Signal. (2020, April 9). Drexel.edu. https://drexel.edu/news/archive/2020/april/creative-insight-triggers-neural-reward

Adler, T. (2020, May 28). One in 10 small business owners contemplating suicide. Small Business UK. https://smallbusiness.co.uk/one-in-10-small-business-owners-contemplating-suicide-2550426/

Suicide by occupation, England - Office for National Statistics. (2011). Ons.gov.uk. https://www.ons.gov.uk/peoplepopulationandcommunity/birthsdeathsand marriages/deaths/articles/suicidebyoccupation/england2011to2015

Peters, P. S. (2012). The chimp paradox. Vermilion.

Hoshi, Y., Huang, J., Kohri, S., Iguchi, Y., Naya, M., Okamoto, T., & Ono, S. (2011). Recognition of human emotions from cerebral blood flow changes in the frontal region: a study with event-related near-infrared spectroscopy. Journal of Neuroimaging, 21(2), e94-e101.

Coelho, H. F., Canter, P. H., & Ernst, E. (2007). Mindfulness-based cognitive therapy: evaluating current evidence and informing future research. Journal of consulting and clinical psychology, 75(6), 1000.

9. The Art of Learning

The Pareto Principle in Language Learning - The 80:20 Rule. (2017, June 29). Bilingua. https://bilingua.io/the-pareto-principle-in-language-learning-the-8020-rule

Zhan, L., Guo, D., Chen, G., & Yang, J. (2018). Effects of repetition learning on associative recognition over time: Role of the hippocampus and prefrontal cortex. Frontiers in human neuroscience, 12, 277.

Kolb, D. A. (2007). The Kolb learning style inventory. Boston, MA: Hay Resources Direct.

Abu-Rabia, S., & Sanitsky, E. (2010). Advantages of bilinguals over monolinguals in learning a third language. Bilingual Research Journal, 33(2), 173-199.

10. Coaching & Mentoring

Connor, M., & Pokora, J. (2017). EBOOK: Coaching and mentoring at work: Developing effective practice. McGraw-Hill Education (UK).

www.vernard.net. (2017, December 14). 1-to-1 Coaching. ActionCOACH. https://www.actioncoach.com/business-coaching-programs/one-to-one/

11. Building a Shed

Hall, D., James, D., & Marsden, N. (2012). Marginal gains: Olympic lessons in high performance for organisations. HR Bulletin: Research and Practice, 7(2), 9-13.

Hutchinson, M. (2015). Faster: the obsession, science and luck behind the world's fastest cyclists. Bloomsbury.

Learn More About BNI | Business Network International. (2019, May 2). BNI. https://www.bni.com/about

Do Givers Get Ahead? (n.d.). Greater Good. Retrieved July 24, 2022, from https://greatergood.berkeley.edu/article/item/do_givers_get_ahead

Dunbar, R. I. (1993). Coevolution of neocortical size, group size and language in humans. Behavioral and brain sciences, 16(4), 681-694.

Vitale, J., & Hibbler, B. (2006). Meet and grow rich: How to easily create and operate your own "Mastermind" group for health, wealth, and more. John Wiley & Sons.

Karinthy, F. (1929). Chain-links. Everything is different, 21-26.

12. Increase Productivity by 30%

Tidd, J., & Bessant, J. R. (2020). Managing innovation: integrating technological, market and organizational change. John Wiley & Sons.

Environments, I. (n.d.). How multiple monitors affects productivity and wellbeing. Www.ie-Uk.com. Retrieved July 23, 2022, from https://www.ie-uk.com/blog/how-multiple-monitors-affects-productivity-and-wellbeing

Hale, R., & Whitlam, P. (1997). Practical problem solving & decision making: an integrated approach. Kogan Page Publishers.

Jawbone: From Innovative to Insolvent. (n.d.). California Management Review Insights. https://cmr.berkeley.edu/2018/04/jawbone-startup-failure/

Inside Bill's Brain: Decoding Bill Gates | Netflix Official Site. (n.d.). Www.netflix.com. Retrieved July 24, 2022, from https://www.netflix.com/gb/title/80184771

Carson, R. (1962). Silent Spring. Penguin Books.

Crutzen, P., Molina, M., & Rowland, F. S. (2016). Nobel Prize in Chemistry in 1995. Paul J. Crutzen, 239.

13. Going Green

Electric Dreams: Green Vehicles Cheaper Than Petrol. (n.d.). DLG Corporate Corporate Website. https://www.directlinegroup.co.uk/en/news/brand-news/2020/29062020.html

Ekins, P. (2018). Final report of the high-level panel of the European decarbonisation pathways initiative.

Smarter heating controls research program. (n.d.). Retrieved July 23, 2022, from https://assets.publishing.service.gov.uk/government/uploads/system/uploads/attachment_data/file/254877/smarter_heating_controls_research_programme_overview.pdf

Mandlem, K. et al. (2020). Energy efficiency effectiveness of smart thermostat based BEMS. Energy Engineering. 117. 165-183. 10.32604/EE.2020.011406.

Why we're trying to help our customers use less gas this winter. (n.d.). Octopus Energy. Retrieved July 23, 2022, from https://octopus.energy/blog/winter-workout-helping-customers-reduce-gas/

14. The Business of Students

Young Enterprise & Young Money. (n.d.). https://www.young-enterprise.org.uk/

Ries, E. (2011). The lean startup: How constant innovation creates radically successful businesses. Portfolio Penguin, Cop.

Belbin, M. (2004). Belbin team roles. Belbin Team Roles.

Myers, I. (1962). The Myers Briggs type indicator: Manual. Palo Alto, CA: Consulting Psychologists Press.

Strategyzer AG. (2019). Strategyzer | Canvases. Strategyzer.com. https://www.strategyzer.com/canvas

Macht, S. A., & Ball, S. (2016). "Authentic Alignment" – a new framework of entrepreneurship education. Education+ Training.

15. The Importance of Work

Blanchard, K. H., & Bowles, S. M. (1998). Gung ho! William Morrow And Company, Inc.

Blasi, J. R., Freeman, R. B., Mackin, C., & Kruse, D. L. (2008). Creating a bigger pie? The effects of employee ownership, profit sharing, and stock options on workplace performance (No. w14230). National Bureau of Economic Research.

John Lewis. (2019). John Lewis Partnership - Employee ownership. Johnlewispartnership.co.uk.https://www.johnlewispartnership.co.uk/work/employee-ownership.html

Hegarty, S. (2020, February 28). The boss who put everyone on 70K. BBC News. https://www.bbc.co.uk/news/stories-51332811

Kahneman, D., & Deaton, A. (2010). High income improves evaluation of life but not emotional well-being. Proceedings of the National Academy of Sciences, 107(38), 16489-16493.

Killingsworth, M. A. (2021). Experienced well-being rises with income, even above $75,000 per year. Proceedings of the National Academy of Sciences, 118(4), e2016976118.

Algoe, S. B., Dwyer, P. C., Younge, A., & Oveis, C. (2020). A new perspective on the social functions of emotions: Gratitude and the witnessing effect. Journal of Personality and Social Psychology, 119(1), 40.

16. Do you Drink Milk?

Collins, J. (2001). Good to great: Why some companies make the leap...and others don't. Random House.

Robert Hogan Listed As One of the Greatest Living Psychologists. (2018, July 2). Hogan Assessments.https://www.hoganassessments.com/blog/new-study-lists-robert-hogan-as-one-of-the-greatest-living-psychologists

Jones, R.J., Woods, S.A., and Guillaume, Y.R.F. (2016), The effectiveness of workplace coaching: A meta-analysis of learning and performance outcomes from coaching. J Occup Organ Psychol, 89: 249-277. https://doi.org/10.1111/joop.12119

17. Wash your hands!

Atul Gawande. (2011). The checklist manifesto: How to get things right. Profile Books.

Center For The Advancement Of Health. (2008, January 25). Handwashing can reduce diarrhea episodes by about one third. ScienceDaily. Retrieved July 22, 2022 from www.sciencedaily.com/releases/2008/01/080122203221.htm

How to Avoid Catastrophe. (2011, April). Harvard Business Review. https://hbr.org/2011/04/how-to-avoid-catastrophe

18. Hi, I'm Dan!

Southon, M., & West, C. (2008). Sales on a beermat. Random House Business.

Phd, R. B. (2021). INFLUENCE, NEW AND EXPANDED UK: the psychology of persuasion. Harpercollins.

Presentation Content Development & Delivery Coaching. (n.d.). Dan Bond Presentation. Retrieved July 24, 2022, from https://danbondpresentation.co.uk/

Blanchard, K. H., & Bowles, S. M. (2011). Raving fans! A revolutionary approach to customer service. Harpercollins.

Eisenberger, N. I., Lieberman, M. D., & Williams, K. D. (2003). Does rejection hurt? An fMRI study of social exclusion. Science, 302(5643), 290-292.

The Benjamin Franklin Effect: How to Build Rapport by Asking for Favors – Effectiviology. (n.d.). https://effectiviology.com/benjamin-franklin-effect/

Cherry, K. (2006, November 15). Heuristics and Cognitive Biases. Verywell Mind; https://www.verywellmind.com/what-is-a-heuristic-2795235

Eisenberger, N. I., Lieberman, M. D., & Williams, K. D. (2003). Does rejection hurt? An fMRI study of social exclusion. Science, 302(5643), 290-292.

19. Herman the German

Seth Godin | Science behind The Art of Marketing. (n.d.). Www.youtube.com. Retrieved July 23, 2022, from https://www.youtube.com/watch?v=r7lpZL9WRL0

Mcrae, J. (2013). Stand-up marketing. John Mcrae.

Rupini, R. V., & Nandagopal, R. (2015). A study on the influence of senses and the effectiveness of sensory branding. Journal of Psychiatry, 18(2), 236.

Blanchard, K. H., & Bowles, S. M. (2011). Raving fans! A revolutionary approach to customer service. Harpercollins.

Heppell, M. (2014). How to be brilliant: change your ways in 90 days! Pearson.

20. Down at the Police Station

Veal, A. J. (2022). The 4-day work-week: the new leisure society? Leisure Studies, 1-16.

Mogilner, C., & Norton, M. I. (2016). Time, money, and happiness. Current Opinion in Psychology, 10, 12–16. https://doi.org/10.1016/j.copsyc.2015.10.018

21. Why my GP is amazing

England, N. (2019). NHS England» GP online services: the key benefits. England.nhs.uk. https://www.england.nhs.uk/gp-online-services/learning-so-far/key-benefits/

Ong, Y. K., & Chee, G. (2005). Infections of the external ear. Ann Acad Med Singapore, 34(4), 330-4.

Author Bio

I describe myself as a family man, a triathlete, and an entrepreneur. I'm enthusiastic about life and find it hard to sit still. I've written this book to help business owners who are constantly looking for answers. I started my first business in 2003 and it has been a rollercoaster of learning from my own mistakes. When it comes to mistakes I've always turned to science in my quest for answers. It's this quest that led me to realise there are many ways we can apply science to our business problems.

My day job is running a small accountancy practice that employs nine staff members and focuses on the SME sector. The practice uses the latest technology to provide an efficient approach to managing client record keeping. I'm also the Financial Director for a local letting agency and I own a small property portfolio. I trained as a computer programmer and ran a web development agency for over ten years before starting the accountancy practice with my wife in 2012. I have been working for Northumbria University as an Associate Lecturer since 2011, teaching subjects such as Graduate Enterprise,

Entrepreneurship & Creativity, E-business, Innovation, and the government-backed Help2Grow program. I have guest lectured on executive MBA programs and acted as a business mentor.

In my personal life, I'm a mad keen triathlete and love going away in my campervan. I travel across the UK in my van with my wife and two boys, taking part in triathlon races.